A Theology of Dating

A Theology of Dating:
The Partial Shadow of Marriage

Copyright © 2022 by Ryul J. Kwon

Published by Overflowing Joy
   #402, Yelim Bldg, 9, Supyo-ro 2-gil, Jung-gu,
   Seoul, 04554, Republic of Korea

Publisher: Young-Ran Kang
Editor: Hye-Mi Kang, Ji-Yeon Kwon
Design: TRINITY
Marketing & Management: Jin-Ho Lee

E-mail: atfeel@hanmail.net
Facebook: https://www.facebook.com/publisherjoy

The first edition was published on March 4, 2022.
Originally this book was published in Korean in 2020.

ISBN 979-11-89303-67-9(03190)

A guideline
for lovers
who dream of
the kingdom
of God

A THEOLOGY OF DATING
The Partial Shadow of Marriage

Ryul J. Kwon

샘솟는
기쁨

A Theological Framework on Dating and Marriage

Have you found yourself being parents with younger members of your family, or being pastor surrounded by youth in your church, asked with intriguing questions such as "How will I court and date the one I like most?" and "Would you please teach to write a love letter?" Cliché, as "experience is the best teacher," is commonly the tutelage in the curiosity stage of our new generation. That would be among the risk factors why the premarital relationship has been a failure to most young people. Here comes a peculiar book with an author who has tenably believed that "God is love," and when you have loved Him first and above all, to love others is a divine reflection and demonstration of His Word and Work on Love.

And, usual romantic expressions – "I love you," "Will you be my lover?" and "Will you marry me?" – are not just emotional bywords that lead couples to embrace easily relationships and commitments intended only for marriage and married life. Hence, the book offers and guides us to define and clarify those expressions at the spiritual and moral levels. While it is true, as observed by many practitioners and pastors, too, that most works within this particular field deal mainly with prevailing psychological observations and evaluations without considering what – why biblical and theological researches can contribute to the study and research. Answers to questions such "How Can We Define Love?", "Is Love an Emotion?" and "Is Love a Will?" will definitely demarcate views and opinions between what community of psychologists and pastoral ministries have adhered to. Thus, the author recalled and employed much for his study of those biblical concepts and models. Thereby he made a theological framework on dating and marriage.

Moreover, on the theological and missional aspects, he argues for the necessity of biblical doctrine on premarital and marital relationships – to learn God did not only institute marriage but exemplified it and demonstrated how He is covenantally married to His people; in our New Testament concept, Christ being betrothed to the church. Furthermore, he has delineated relevant standpoints on the dos and don'ts while engaged with someone, even to instances of dating non-Christians. Within the same vein, he renders diagnostic observations and evaluations of true symptoms of love involving physical contacts; exposing sexual desire and spiritual desire as subsequently diagnosed.

According to him, dating and marriage should bear a mindset that is grounded on the doctrinal instructions of God's Word; (for youth pastors and counselors) the biblical-theological framework should be serving as groundwork and guidelines for dating and marriage.

While reading this work, I seemed to seek a farm lot where I could start planting exotic flowers and therewith cultured the best flowery garden people would be amazingly asking how I did it. Likewise, another impression I have on it is that I traveled with an interesting guy who is certain that we will have a journey safe and sound due to the roadmap he is holding – elaborated with details about each landmark en route to our destiny. Likewise, the author having a work stint in the campus ministry of Student for Christ and frequently serving as a lecturer on pre-marriage courses is so qualified to write on youth talks, their significant issues, and concerns such as dating and marriage (on love, courtship, and marriage).

Hopefully, praying that young people in our congregation will find this book very helpful, particularly in our ministries for youth and yuppies in the church; also finding it biblically informative and missionally applicable to youth pastors whose interests are in this field.

Antonio C. San Jose
President and Professor of Theology
Immanuel Theological Seminary
January 20, 2022

Dating Principles in the Bible

When I was dating before marriage, I was often teased. My friends used to say, "What kind of dating are you doing? That kind of dating doesn't work these days." I have heard so many times that dating should be romantic and church sisters like it too.

But the dating they teased was the reason that moved my daily life. It was a date to prepare our marriage, dreaming of the kingdom of God with her. Rather than looking at each other, I wanted it to be a date where the two looked together in the same direction. I wanted to share a date for the kingdom of God and the church.

My dating sense was poor, but I got married very early compared to my peers. Even before graduating from college, I had a "grand" wedding with the blessings of both families. I finished the rest of my undergraduate life while married, and since then, I have been walking the path of a minister.

When I was dating, the best dating textbook was the Bible. Besides the Bible, I read other books from time to time. This book, *A Theology of Dating: The Partial Shadow of Marriage,* frequently cites not only theological books but also the humanities, counseling, and psychology. However, the essence of dating and its direction were found only in the Bible. I was able to understand the principles of dating by extracting them from the Bible texts related to marriage.

My theology of dating is a guide for lovers dreaming of the kingdom of God. Dating and marriage are the daily routines of God's kingdom that has already come, and are looking forward to His kingdom that will be consummated in the future. Since every moment of dating touches His kingdom, it must be understood, at least in the context of the kingdom of God. All of our daily life, as well as dating, should be focused on His kingdom which is to come in the future.

Dating is the best area for Christian young adults showing that they are different from non-Christians. God wants their dating to prove who He is. God is looking for lovers who are willing to receive His rule in matters of dating that are directly related to their fundamental desires. God is waiting for couples who want to give to His sovereignty the realm of dating they hate to give up.

For such couples, *A Theology of Dating* is a practical guide. First, I will examine what dating and marriage are similar to and different from each other, and establish the essence and concept of love based on the Bible. I will present the principles for dating based on the Bible and doctrine, and will elaborately argue that loving God and loving mate are inseparable. We will also discuss couples' physical touch and the symptoms of love, and look at the realities and actual examples of the church in relation to dating. Dating is the preparatory stage that eventually leads to marriage. Although this book is a theology of "dating," I will conclude after briefly discussing marriage and married life.

In particular, I expect church ministers to use *A Theology of Dating* appropriately. They can experience the principles of the life of faith as well as the issues of dating. Moreover, this book covers in detail how we should love God and what His love for us is like. I am sure that it will be of great benefit to young people's dating guidance and the life of faith of church members. Moreover, there are questions for sharing and application in each chapter for use in small group meetings.

About two years ago, I first wrote this book in Korean titled 「연애 신학」, which many Korean Christians like to read. So Chapter 6 might be specific to the Korean church situation. Please read this book with that in mind. Now I have joyfully translated it into English for English-speaking readers.

Finally, I would like to thank some people. I express my sincere gratitude to CEO Young-Ran Kang of Overflowing Joy (샘솟는기쁨) for publishing the contents of my lecture as a book. And I give profound thanks for reading the manuscript and writing the foreword, to Professor Antonio C. San Jose of Immanuel Theological Seminary.

I want to express my gratitude to Senior Pastor Young-Sun Kim and all the saints in Purunsup Church and all the staff of Saegyaero Hospital in Busan, who are my sermon listeners and co-workers. Also, I express my hearty appreciation to Staff Eunji Rebekah Lee of Student For Christ, who read the manuscript and sent honest comments. Finally, I dedicate this book to my beloved wife Mi-Ae Son, my companion in life. All glory to God!

Ryul J. Kwon
January 20, 2022

Chapter 1.

The Basis For
A Theology of Dating

Sarah, now let's get to the conclusion. Was it difficult to read because the content was long? Please be a little more patient. As I said before, the purpose of dating is not love or marriage. I think the purpose is in this word. "So, whether you eat or drink, or whatever you do, do all to the glory of God" (1 Cor. 10:31).[1] I am sure that the way we glorify God is by testifying to the kingdom of God.

This is the biggest reason why I love you. I love you because of the earnest desire to participate in the kingdom of God with you, who respond very sensitively to His word. Your tall height and outstanding beauty may be the catalyst that makes me love you more, but they are not the reason itself for loving you.

At some point, I made a decision. I mean, I want to love you. Do you understand now? If you still don't understand, read this letter several times. Love is by no means a form of feeling that comes naturally, and I don't want to love like that. The feeling of love that was naturally created in that way will change someday. For example, it would change into the disappointment that comes from being under-excited than at first.

★

1) Unless otherwise indicated, Scripture quotations are from the ESV Bible in this book.

After that, people would think again. "Is my love for this person growing cold?" Or "Do I need to keep dating because I can't love him/her anymore?" If you look carefully at these words, they downplay love as a kind of feeling.

Feelings may or may not arise. But love is not like that. Love is the determination and conviction to do so. Then an excited state of feeling will one day follow. However, the feelings created by doing so do not last long. Although it is the result of love, feelings are feelings. If you don't believe this, ask the married people whether the feelings they had at first persist or not.

The important thing is that there is nothing wrong with falling in love, even if the excitement subsides.

Sarah, I'm sorry that I also don't have a feeling of love just as you do. Moreover, it's not like I am in a state where I must see you every day with the height of feelings as in puberty.

I'm not saying this because I don't love you. If you still think that way, I must be a little disappointed.

I have decided that I will love you and try to do so. The reason is simple because I'm convinced that we are precious co-workers who sincerely want to live for the kingdom of God. I really want to study the Bible with you, and I want to continue our relationship sharing about issues of faith. Also, it is my heart and confession that I want to continue a rich relationship, expecting to experience the thrill of feelings.

If God leads us, our relationship is going for the glory of God. As a result, marriage would be given as a "gift." So I decided not to obsess over the result. If we become obsessed with it, we may miss out on what God wants us to do now. I leave the result entirely to God, and I try to experience His grace with you every day. (the rest omitted)

This is part of a love letter that I wrote before marriage. Sarah in the letter is my wife now. Sarah is her English name. I chanced to find this letter while writing a manuscript for *A Theology of Dating*. Believe it or not, I was writing the letter nonstop for six hours on Friday, June 18, 2004, from 7:18 a.m. to 1:16 p.m. That's why the letter is incredibly long. I was in my mid-20s at that time.

Even reading it now, this letter is like a sermon or lecture. I am so unfamiliar with myself that I wonder what I was thinking when I wrote it. If I were to write it again now, I don't know if I could display that level of spiritual determination or vigor. Showing this letter to my wife just made her laugh. She made fun of me, saying, "You loved me so much that you don't want to lose me."

I think my appearance and way of thinking in my mid-20s were so unique. I have been to a movie theater with her for the first time in my life. I realized through her that my dating sense was so poor. Like any other college student, I've never had an exhilarating date, and I've never known what girls like and want. When I was dating, she often used to say, "It's the first time I've met someone like you out of all the men I've ever met."

Thinking about it now, she must have been very frustrated at that time because she was excellent at actual dating. Nevertheless, she said that she experienced the grace of being filled with the Holy Spirit deeply while having an extraordinary dating with me. So I am convinced that our marriage was possible by the grace of God. No matter how much I think, it's just amazing that a woman decided to share her life with me. I was always thinking I was not appealing to any woman.

The content of this book, *A Theology of Dating*, is based on the love letter I wrote for 6 hours at that time. All the gist of what I'm trying to say is almost contained in that letter. I don't know what I was thinking when dating like that. Maybe I made a woman burdensome, but I think I will do the same if I have to date again now. That is why I have had a clear view of dating since my mid-20s. It is the content that I have established in my way before God through my failed dating experiences.

Friends in Christ who once read my love letter sent various feedbacks. Some were sarcastic, saying, "Your love letter is like building castles in the air," while others read it repeatedly with a copy of it. Someone even posted on her blog without permission. Anyway, I remember being confused because the reactions were more varied than expected.

The contents of the letter may sound like building castles in the air to many people. But for me, at least, it was a reality that moved my daily life and dating. It is the same even now that we are married. The kingdom of God and His vision are leading our married life. From my mid-20s, I realized where dating and marriage should face, based on the Bible.

I don't know the so-called secular dating methodology. I'm more adept at that method than dating before marriage, but I'm still close to an outsider compared to a professional instructor in that field. If you expect such content from *A Theology of Dating*, it is better to give up in advance. Even if it sounds a bit absurd, like building castles in the air, I would appreciate it if you listen carefully with patience.

I know some readers have been shocked from the beginning of this book. Some readers will taunt it like a date that does not fit with this age at all, while others will sarcastically say that it is just a theory by a minister who does not know the reality. Any feedback is welcome. I've already heard those words countless times, so now I never mind. As I said before, it may be unrealistic and mere theory to them, but at least to me, the content of the letter is a living reality that moves dating and marriage.

I think the gospel we believe is also like that. To some, it sounds like building castles in the air, but to others, it's all they risk their lives for. The cross and resurrection of Christ, the kingdom of God and His vision based on them, the confession of faith based on the "rock," and the power of God seem to be heard like that by more church members than I think. It seems that they don't feel it in their bones.

We believe dating and marriage are directly related to our daily lives. But we would think of the kingdom of God and His gospel as if they were separate from our daily lives. Still, we must not take that phenomenon for granted! Although everyone feels and thinks that way, Christians shouldn't force themselves to think so.

The content of the Bible, which we absolutely trust, says that all our daily lives are in the kingdom of God. In other words, our everyday lives without God's rule cannot exist at all. The same goes for dating and marriage. In particular, dating, which is directly related to the fundamental desires of the unmarried, must be under God's rule. Therefore, if the content of my love letter is based on the kingdom of God and His gospel, it is not a view of dating that is separated from daily life, but rather one that is directly related to all daily life in the kingdom of God.

At the very least, the Christian view of dating should be distinguished from the world's view. Our sexual reactions and attraction towards each other are no different from theirs. Still, the basis for dating and what it aims for must be something they cannot imitate. Now we can't back down anymore, and we must seek an actual conversion to the Christian view of dating. We must all work together so that the dating towards God's kingdom and His vision may be natural, at least to us. What would you like to prove that you are a Christian couple different from the world?

 ## No Difference in Dating Standards

Young people of marriageable age have clear standards for mate selection. In many cases, men have standards that their future spouse must have a pretty face, a good body, or a good home environment. Women also have standards that their future spouse should be good-natured with a handsome face, have a good sense of humor, or be able to calm women's hearts.

Putting these words together means that once the person is attracted to me, I can think of him/her as a future spouse. In other words, I would self-centeredly think before starting a relationship. I can start a relationship only when the person reacts the way I want and meets the standards I set.

But the problem is that even the church's young people start dating that way. Just like non-Christians, they have their criteria for choosing a mate. Some sisters have the standard that a brother must have faith in Jesus, have economic power, and be good-looking. Some brothers have the standard that a sister has faith and all the family must live a life of faith. In addition to that, there are several other criteria.

In this way, the church's young adults have "clear" standards for dating and marriage. Of course, as children of God, we must have a clear view of dating. But the problem is that it's not that different from the way non-Christians start dating. Trying to date a Christian person is a good thing. But that's just a vague premise and doesn't seem to be different from the way people in the world start dating.

You might be asking yourself, "What's wrong with that?" When you strongly argue, "How can we start a relationship with someone we don't like?" I'm not firmly opposed to it either. I want to suggest that you think about it from a different angle just for once. The idea that you think it is natural is not taken for granted. It is a relatively recent occurrence from a historical point of view.

Once you look at the Bible, you can't find a dating method like to-day. Human first dating and marriage were directly joined together by God (Gen. 2:22-24). The dating and marriage that have been intro-duced since then are mostly determined by the parents' intentions or external factors rather than the romantic love of the parties involved. So was the meeting between Isaac and Rebekah (24:3-67), and so was the meeting between Jacob and Rachel (29:6-30). There was even a law that, if a married older brother died without a son, the younger brother had to marry his sister-in-law and inherit it (Deut. 25:5).

Besides the Bible, it was no different in general history. The idea that I decide whom I love is a change that only occurred in the 20th century. Until then, they had little rights to decide about dating and marriage; instead, they were determined by family decisions, match-makers, and other social factors.[2] The current dating method is a historically new phenomenon in line with the characteristics of modern culture.

My point is that the concept of dating that we take for granted is not originally taken for granted. If so, you should ask. How should Christian dating be different from the way of the world? Of course, I don't think the outward way in the Bible is the right answer for all ages. Figuratively speaking, it is similar to how the external method of administering the covenant is different between the Old and New Testaments.[3]

Nevertheless, we must remember that Christian dating and marriage have an unchangeable nature and standards. We should at least reconsider self-centric dating and marriage. However, it does not

★

2) Erich Fromm, *The Art of Loving* (London: Bradford & Dickens, Drayton House, 1956), 2.

3) The same covenant of grace was administered through promises, prophecies, sacrifices, and circumcision in the Old Testament, and through the sacraments of baptism and the Lord's Supper in the New Testament. For more details, see the Westminster Larger Catechism, Questions 33-35.

mean you should kill your thoughts and only date and marry someone your parents choose. I want to point out that external factors play a significant role in Christian dating and marriage. The external factors are the Christian standards that are fundamentally different from the world's dating.

Two Perspectives on Dating and Marriage

There are two perspectives to approach Christian dating and marriage. Depending on the researchers, it may be further subdivided, but as a field minister, I divide it into two broad categories. One is from a developmental psychology perspective. This is a way to study how we interact with the opposite sex (unmarried or married), especially as Christians, in adolescence (or childhood) and adulthood, regarding dating and marriage as a developmental process like non-Christian researchers.

The other is a biblical-theological approach. This is a method of deriving the characteristics and definition of dating and marriage based thoroughly on the Bible and doctrine, especially a method of studying marriage's ultimate substance and purpose. Real-life examples of dating and marriage are also covered in part. It, too, takes its principles from the Bible and applies them in ways that control our sinful nature.

The main focus of this book is a biblical-theological perspective. So I named my research a "theology of dating" with the intention of making it unique. All areas of our lives are related to the fulfillment of God's vision. Therefore, Christian dating and marriage must also be understood in the context of the fulfillment of God's vision. His vision is for the whole world to be consummated as the sinless kingdom of God and for the gospel of the cross to be glorified throughout the earth.

Dating and marriage are the top concerns of all young people. Those are also areas where they most want to be free. I don't want to leave young people to compromise with their desires in this area. If you are a young man who really wants to live for the glory of God, you must change even your basic desire to be God-centered. *A Theology of Dating* provides guidance in this area.

Finally, I will briefly discuss the interrelationship of these two perspectives. Just because the main concern is the biblical-theological approach, it doesn't mean that I ignore or deny the developmental psychology approach. However, I would like to emphasize that the biblical-theological approach should form the core and the overall framework, and the developmental psychology approach should be partially utilized. No matter how excellent the latter approach is, if it does not address the fulfillment of God's vision and the ultimate substance of marriage, it will only lead to preoccupation with each other's reaction mechanisms. Therefore, *A Theology of Dating* is a must to guide Christian dating and marriage.

I am very interested in Christian dating and marriage. Contrary to how I look, I started dating early, and I got married at the age of my mid-20s. Seeing that I have friends who are still unmarried over 40, it seems that I got married earlier than my peers. Of course, it's not because I'm good, but because of God's grace and thanks to the compassionate heart of my lover (now wife) at that time.

Also, from an early age, I was very fond of the Bible and doctrine. While I was dating, I always looked for the principles and methods in the Bible. Surprisingly, the principles of Christian dating were hidden throughout the Bible. Not just of dating but also marriage. The principles of marriage are more explicitly stated. So I am convinced that the best textbook for dating and marriage is the Bible.

My concerns about biblical dating began about 20 years ago. From then on, I first conducted clinical trials on myself. I started to organize the parts I realized by combining them with the Bible and doctrine. They are not entirely original, though, and I partly borrowed the language of previous researchers. In any case, it is called "theology of dating" because it has its system and is the result of organizing it from a biblical-theological point of view.

So, what does the expression "theology of dating" mean? The word *theology* combines two Greek words, *theos* (θεός) which is for "God" and *logos* (λόγος) which is for "word." Theology can be translated into two meanings: "God says to us" or "We say about God."[4] There-fore, a theology of dating means "God says to us through dating" or "We say about God through dating." Then a young Christian man and woman must listen to what God is saying through their dating. At the same time, their dating itself must be a journey to witness God.

In former times, I read John Piper's *This Momentary Marriage*. Each time I turned the pages, I was truly amazed because his view was almost identical to my usual view of marriage. He derived the ultimate substance and purpose of marriage from the Bible and devel-oped a theology of marriage in the context of Christ and the church.[5] Putting in my words, Piper listens to God through marriage and un-derstands marriage itself as a journey of witnessing God and a process of sanctification.

Therefore, Christian dating and marriage are fundamentally dif-ferent from those of the world. Above all, that's because God always beneficially intervenes on unmarried or married couples, and because God sovereignly works by His providence for dating and marriage ac-cording to His purpose. In this context, dating and marriage different from the world's must be restored quickly among us! In particular, ministers should make every effort to guide the church's young people to adapt their fundamental desires to the holy view of dating.

★
4) 유해무, 『개혁교의학』 (고양: 크리스찬다이제스트, 1997), 21.
5) John Piper, *This Momentary Marriage* (Wheaton, Illinois: Crossway Books, 2009), 24-25.

So, whether you eat or drink, or whatever you do, do all to the glory of God. (1 Cor. 10:31)

This verse is very familiar to Christians. The context before and after is about eating sacrifices. When dealing with things sacrificed to idols, Paul urges them to "eat whatever is set before you without raising any question on the ground of conscience," or not to eat "for the sake of the one who informed you." It is not important whether they eat or not eat, but he urges them to eat or drink for the glory of God.

I am not here to discuss the issue of things sacrificed to idols. I want to pay attention to the expression "whatever you do" in verse 31. The apostle Paul did not limit our life for the glory of God to just eating and drinking things sacrificed to idols. He says, "whether you eat or drink, or whatever you do, do all to the glory of God."

So, what are some life situations corresponding to "whatever you do?" Even if we limit them to the church in Corinth at that time, we can think of various kinds of situations. They lived in numerous life situations, including fornication, lawsuits, marriage, idolatry, the Lord's Supper, and abuse of spiritual gifts. They realized that all those had to be solved for the glory of God according to Paul's teaching.

Is this verse only given to the church in Corinth? A person who thinks so disregards the Word of God. The words of the Bible are universal, applicable to all peoples of all times unless the context is limited. Therefore, this is the Lord's command that applies equally to us today.

Now, I will apply dating and marriage to the life situation corresponding to "whatever you do" in verse 31. Since the issue of marriage was given a lot of attention at that time, it is not at all a problem to apply it to Christian dating and marriage issues today.

The Couple in the Same Direction!

"Love does not consist in gazing at each other but in looking outward together in the same direction."[6]

This is a phrase from Antoine de Sainte-Exupery's *Wind, Sand and Stars*. It is a sentence that gives excellent insight into Christian dating because it tells the direction of love well. (Of course, the original context is about friendship.) Not to mention non-Christians, even Christian young adults, are accustomed to gazing at each other when dating. But this inevitably distorts the essence of love. Because God is love (1 John 4:8), all love is given meaning only when we are directed

A Theology of Dating

★

6) Antoine de Saint-Exupery, *Wind, Sand and Stars,* trans. Lewis Galantiere (New York: Reynal & Hitchcock, 1939), 288.

to Him. That includes not only the dating of young people, but also the love between husband and wife.

So, where should our love indicate? In particular, where should Christian young adults look when dating? If these questions make you feel awkward or even offended, your faith definitely has a problem. Why? Because reacting in such a way proves that you are thinking of yourself separately from God in this aspect.

This book is not about how a Christian single man and woman can succeed in dating. Moreover, it is not a book that analyzes the different characteristics of men and women by type and suggests how to fall in love accordingly. You can refer to the books of writers who are "well-versed" in dating for such content.

My focus is on the ultimate direction of Christian dating and marriage. In addition, I will cover in detail how the direction affects the current dating and marriage, and therefore how to start a relationship.

Let's start with a few questions. If you are single reading this book, for what purpose do you want to date? Of course, I require more than the answer that the purpose of dating is marriage. If you are married, what perspective would you like to advise unmarried couples?

Does this sound like a vague and old-fashioned question? Let me ask more specific questions. Have you ever seriously considered the relationship between dating and our faith? Have you thought about what Christian dating means in the context of the kingdom of God? Also, have you ever thought about the meaning and ultimate direction of Christian marriage and married life based on the Bible?

Perhaps you are reminded of the word, "whatever you do, do all to the glory of God" (1 Cor. 10:31). But it is not good to be content with spitting that word out like a parrot. You must be able to answer in detail how you are actually dating and what kind of marriage you are dreaming of for the glory of God.

Young people remembering that word are still hopeful because they have the spiritual sense of remembering the words of God. It seems that they increasingly have their own way of dating and marriage. Even some Christian young people hate that dating and marriage have anything to do with the Bible.

But we can't back off any longer. I want Christian young adults to long for the glory of God and to be captivated by His kingdom. I hope that an actual conversion will occur in their view of dating. What is the surest sign by which our young people can be distinguished from their worldly friends? The view of dating, which is directly related to their fundamental desires, is "fitting in the kingdom of God."

Does that idea seem too unrealistic and impossible? By no means! Because of the faults of the ministers who failed to guide their dating properly, it only seems naive. It's not too late now. Young adult pastors and older generations should pray and unite for a "holy revival" to occur in the intense desire of young people. Moreover, we must remember that converting their view of dating is a great way to renew the church. Why? Because the church's holiness largely depends on the Christian view of dating and marriage, which is distinct from the world.

 ## Everyday Life's Direction

Everyday life is directly related to the kingdom of God. This is not a matter to be agreed or disagreed. Our very existence cannot be separated from the kingdom of God because God is the creator of the whole world.

But in Genesis 3, sin entered the kingdom of God. Since then, the concept of His kingdom has been differentiated. It was originally a "one" concept but was cracked due to sin, creating a realm where God's rule was not perfect. Of course, this realm was also permitted under the sovereignty of God. Since this is the common realm of rule shared with the world, it is called God's *universal (or general) rule.* This realm can also be called the kingdom of God in the general sense.

On the other hand, there is a realm where God's whole rule exists. It is the realm of rule through the gospel of the cross, which we call *redemptive rule.* It already started in the form of a promise right after

7) For more details, see Gordon R. Lewis and Bruce A. Demarest, *Integrative Theology, Volume 2: Our Primary Need: Christ's Atoning Provisions* (Grand Rapids, MI: Zondervan, 1990), 71-122.

sin entered (Gen. 3:15). Still, it has been in full-scale progress since the Crucifixion on Calvary 2,000 years ago and especially the resurrection of Christ. For the sake of the redemptive rule, God establishes the church on this earth, and the kingdom of God is expanding day by day through the church. This redemptive rule is God's kingdom that Jesus proclaimed while living on this earth (Mark 1:14-15; Luke 8:1). Because this kingdom of God, which means redemptive rule, is the gospel, it is called the gospel of God's kingdom. Also, because the divine basis for making His kingdom come was fulfilled on the cross (John 19:30), the kingdom of God can never be separated from the gospel of the cross.[8]

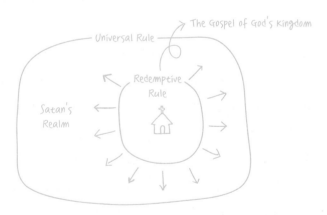

The Conceptual Map of God's Kingdom

---

8) For this reason, the apostles and disciples proclaimed the cross and resurrection events when they preached the gospel. This is because the gospel of God's kingdom that Jesus spoke of is based on those events.

As you can see in *The Conceptual Map of God's Kingdom,* we are living in a time when the kingdom of God (redemptive rule) is expanding through the church. This will continue until the Last Day (the Second Coming). Our everyday lives should be understood in this context. In particular, when young people are dating, they need to keep that in mind as the first principle.

Are we dreaming of the kingdom of God? Do you really live aware that His kingdom, which began since the Resurrection, will be consummated on this earth in the future? We should never think that the "paradise" our souls enter after dying is our final destination.[9] We must have faith that goes beyond the paradise. Our faith is a *temporal* faith. It does not mean secular, but it is a faith "related to the earth we are treading on." Why? Because the kingdom of God will be consummated in the world where we live now. On that day, the entire universe, including the earth, will be transformed (or renewed) into a new heaven and a new earth.

That's why it's so important how we live our daily lives now. Every moment that seems currently meaningless contributes in some way to the completion of the kingdom of God. The kingdom of God does not come based on our obedience and works, but God makes it come through our daily actions. When the Lord comes again, He will "cre-

★

9) After death, our souls will be glorified in paradise (intermediate state), and finally will be clothed in a glorious resurrection body on this earth at the Second Coming of the Lord.

ate" a new heaven and a new earth. But He will not destroy the world and build it up on the traces we have left.

Now I want to ask questions to Christian brothers and sisters: Do you not want to contribute to the completion of the kingdom of God through your only life? How about surrendering your most uncompromising dating to His sovereignty? Don't you want to dream of His kingdom with your lover, captivated by God's love? What about being convinced that only the gospel of the cross is the power of God that determines your view of dating?

Marriage Is a Great Mystery

The best dating guide for Christian young adults is in the Bible. It doesn't mean that books other than the Bible are useless. You can also get useful information about dating through general humanities or counseling psychology books. I also studied counseling but could not complete the M.A. for some reason.

Above all else, we must use the Bible as our guide to dating. There is a mystery about dating that only the Bible can tell. This idea may sound strange, but it is a fact. Of course, the Bible has very few sentences that directly state dating itself. However, based on theological principles, we can derive any number of guidelines for dating from texts related to marriage.

The mystery of marriage lies in the statements of the apostle Paul, Ephesians 5:31-32 (NKJV).

[31] *"For this reason a man shall leave his father and mother and be joined to his wife, and the two shall become one flesh."* [32] This is a great mystery, but I speak concerning Christ and the church.

Verse 31 says that a man leaves his father and mother, is joined to the woman, and becomes one flesh. It is not a verse that Paul himself came up with, but a quotation from Genesis 2:24: "Therefore a man shall leave his father and mother and be joined to his wife, and they shall become one flesh" (NKJV). This verse follows right after God joined together Adam and Eve. That is why it is the Word of God given as a universal law on marriage.

Paul continues with a meaningful statement right after quoting Genesis 2:24. "This is a great mystery, but I speak concerning Christ and the church." After mentioning the marriage between a man and a woman, which God has joined together, he immediately says, "This is a great mystery!" In other words, the marriage relationship between husband and wife is a great mystery.[10] That's why marriage is called a

---

★

10) William Hendriksen and Simon J. Kistemaker, *Exposition of Ephesians,* vol. 7, NTC (Grand Rapids, MI: Baker Book House, 1953–2001), 257. For reference, some scholars interpret "mystery" (v. 32) only as the relationship between Christ and the church according to its usage. However, in the context of the flow, "mystery" refers to verse 31 (Gen. 2:24), and its content (substance) should be interpreted as "Christ and the church." Given this context, I freely accept their interpretations.

"great mystery."

Paul goes on to explain why marriage is called a great mystery. "I speak concerning Christ and the church." That is, through the marriage relationship of husband and wife, the apostle ultimately wants to speak about Christ and the church. Because the marriage ultimately reveals the relationship between Christ and the church, it is a "great mystery."

In other words, the ultimate substance of a marriage relationship is Christ and the church. If Christ and the church are the ultimate *substances,* it means that the marriage relationship is a temporary *shadow.* To borrow John Piper's phrase, the former is the "original" and the latter the "copy."[11]

Here we can find the direction of married life. It means that we should see what Christ and the church look like by looking at the married life of a husband and wife. That is, the mystical union of Christ and the church must be revealed through the secret union between husband and wife. This is the "great mystery" of the marriage the Lord has instituted.

Throughout the Bible, our relationship with God is compared to "husband and wife" (or groom and bride). In addition, the relationship between king and people, father and children, is also expressed between God and us. Nevertheless, the relational metaphor through

★

11) John Piper, *Preparing for Marriage* (Minneapolis, MN: Desiring God, 2018), 21.

which we can recognize the attribute of love most vividly is the marriage relationship between husband and wife. These verses are introduced below:

For your Maker is your husband, the LORD of hosts is his name; . . . (Isa. 54:5)

"Return, faithless people," declares the LORD, "for I am your husband. . . . (Jer. 3:14, NIV)

"And in that day, declares the LORD, you will call me 'My Husband,' . . . (Hos. 2:16)

And Jesus said to them, "Can the wedding guests mourn as long as the bridegroom is with them? . . . (Matt. 9:15)

The one who has the bride is the bridegroom. The friend of the bridegroom, who stands and hears him, rejoices greatly at the bridegroom's voice. . . . (John 3:29)

. . . since I betrothed you to one husband, to present you as a pure virgin to Christ. (2 Cor. 11:2)

As you can see, the Bible continues to compare God and us as husband and wife or groom and bride. If church members were properly aware of the "great mystery" of marriage, the divorce rate would not be this high. If they remember that marriage is a wonderful means to testify to the mystical union of Christ and the church, their attitude toward marriage will change dramatically.

I got married in 2005, but I still lack in that area. Even if my ministry skills seem to improve, I often miss the ultimate direction of marriage. I dare not be sure that church members will be able to discover the beauty of Christ and the church as they watch my married life.

Nevertheless, thanks to the mercy and grace of the Lord, I am writing this book. I would appreciate it if you could treat this book as a self-reflection confession. I make it clear that I am not saying these things because I dated and got married based on the principles of the Bible. Of course, it is true that before marriage, I dated eccentrically in the sight of young people. When I met my beloved (now wife), I endeavored to date with the gospel, studied the Bible together, and often had time to pray. On the first night of our honeymoon, we spent time praying together from midnight to dawn at a prayer center.

Anyway, this book was started by harmonizing the speculations while dating and theological thoughts until now. So I can speak in a more experiential language. Christian marriage is a "great mystery" and should ultimately reveal the relationship between Christ and the church! In theological terms, marriage is an irrevocable covenant. It does not refer to the reality of marriage but the nature of marriage initially intended by God.

 ## Dating Is a Little Mystery

So, what is the relationship between dating and marriage? The interests of unmarried young people are more focused on dating than marriage. As a minister for them, I often feel their longing for dating. Sometimes I arrange a meeting like a blind date. But the failure rate is higher than the success rate that leads to a relationship. The cause of failure in many cases is the influence of the distorted view of dating nowadays.

There is an expression that Christian young adults should not use: "Dating is one thing; marriage is quite another!" The intent of this statement is somewhat understandable. It seems to mean that no matter how much you date, there is only one person who you will get married to. Or maybe it means that when you're immature, you meet the opposite sex just because you love dating, but when you're mature, you'll pull yourself together and meet someone you'll marry.

In any case, dating and marriage cannot be considered separately. It is the same logic: we cannot separate the Christian marriage from the relationship between Christ and the church. In conclusion, dating is the "partial shadow" of marriage. It is a principle similar to this:

marriage is the shadow of the ultimate substance (i.e., the mystical union of Christ and the church). Therefore, the principle of the "little mystery" which is dating can be derived from the "great mystery" which is marriage.

The same principle cannot work between the two. Although dating and marriage look similar, they are entirely different. So dating is the "partial" shadow of marriage. To borrow difficult terms, there is a continuity and a discontinuity between dating and marriage. Let's summarize dating, marriage, and the ultimate substance in a table so that we can see at a glance.

First, let's compare marriage and ultimate substance. If we look at the original nature of marriage that God intended, the ultimate substance and marriage operate on the same principle. But the former is the substance, and the latter is only the shadow. As the table shows,

Dating (Little Mystery)	Marriage (Great Mystery)	Ultimate Substance (Mystical Union)
Unmarried (Brother/Sister)	Husband + Wife	Christ + Church
	Shadow ←⟶ Substance	
Partial Shadow ←⟶ Relative Substance		
Revocable	Irrevocable (There can be exceptions)	Irrevocable Absolutely
Flexible Role	Inflexible Role (There can be exceptions)	Inflexible Role Absolutely

Dating vs. Marriage vs. Ultimate Substance

both contain a mysterious and secret union, are in an irrevocable covenant relationship, and the role of each object of the union is inflexible.

However, the same principle cannot work qualitatively and quantitatively. Why? Because of each attribute of substance and shadow. The substance is perfect, but the shadow is imperfect. While the substance tells the whole thing, the shadow tells only a part. Thus, while we must witness the mystical union of Christ and the church through married life, we cannot manifest it in every aspect perfectly. It is because we, as creatures, partly and temporarily experience the nature of ultimate substance (mystical union) through marriage until we die.

Let us recall what Jesus said during the resurrection debate. "For in the resurrection they neither marry nor are given in marriage, but are like angels in heaven" (Matt. 22:30). When the glorious resurrection takes place on the day of Christ's return, there will be no more marriages. In other words, when the substance of mystical union comes through the glorious resurrection, the present institution of marriage ceases to exist. The substance of that union will appear on that day as the "marriage supper of the Lamb" (Rev. 19:9).

Our Lord, who instituted the marriage in Genesis 2, refers to its abolition in Matthew 22. It means that He wants to ultimately testify to the mystical union between Him and us through the union (marriage) of husband and wife from the beginning. The apostle Paul clearly reveals the Lord's intention in Ephesians 5:31-32.

Now let's compare dating and marriage. There are similarities (continuity) between the two. A man and a woman enjoy a close and intimate relationship with each other. It is an exclusive state in which no third party can intervene "as long as the relationship continues." In general, marriage comes after dating, so marriage is the substance of dating and dating is the partial shadow of marriage. (This is also a discontinuity.) Of course, since marriage is distinct from the ultimate substance, it is always a "relative substance."

However, there are completely distinct aspects (discontinuity). As the table shows, marriage is, in principle, an irrevocable covenant. On the other hand, dating is a temporary relationship that can be broken because it is not a union. That is why during dating, you cannot enjoy the secret relationship (one flesh) of complete exclusivity that you will enjoy in marriage. There is also a difference between the two in revealing the ultimate substance. Marriage has a fixed or inflexible role for each, but dating doesn't necessarily have to do that. As in marriage, the unmarried brother cannot necessarily be the head of the unmarried sister. We will focus on that in Chapter 6.

In summary, dating and marriage have both continuity and discontinuity at the same time. It is continuous in terms of the continuation of intimate relationships, but it is distinctly discontinuous in terms of each essential attribute. For those reasons, and because of the relationship between relative substance and partial shadow, I call dating a "little mystery" since marriage is said to be a "great mystery."

1. Please share honestly about your view of dating or standards for dating.

2. Have you ever thought about the connection between dating and the glory of God?

3. Do you really believe that the kingdom of God, which began in earnest 2,000 years ago, is currently in progress and will be consummated by Christ's return?

4. Christian marriage reveals the relationship between Christ and the church. Would you mind telling specifically in what ways that is so?

5. Please share freely in your words how dating and marriage are similar to and different from each other.

Chapter 2.

Existential Love and Conceptual Love

Now let's get to the really important part. Perhaps the most essential part of this book. How can we define love? This question evokes varying answers for so many people, regardless of religion. Philosophers try to prove what love is with several philosophical concepts. Biologists will explain love as a physical response to hormone secretion. However, psychologists will describe it as an emotional intimacy with each other, usually occurring either unconsciously or consciously.

That shows it is impossible to define what love is in one sentence. How would you like to define love if you are reading this book? Each reader will respond differently, and my answer may be one of many sentences. So, rather than defining love, we describe some aspects of it in our own language.

Nevertheless, I try to make a seemingly reckless attempt. It's impossible to define love in one sentence, so let's look at it from several aspects. We will look at how the Bible describes love because we have to think depending on the complete revelation of the Bible (i.e., revelation-dependent thinking).

The greatest definition of love is found in 1 John 4:7-10.

[7]Beloved, let us love one another, for love is from God, and whoever loves has been born of God and knows God. [8]Anyone who does not love does not know God, because God is love. [9]In this the love of

God was made manifest among us, that God sent his only Son into the world, so that we might live through him. ¹⁰In this is love, not that we have loved God but that he loved us and sent his Son to be the propitiation for our sins.

Pay special attention to the second half of verse 8. ". . . because God is love." As the apostle of love, John asserts God Himself is love. This should be the starting point for everything that defines love. Love is not a conceptual dimension separate from a relational one but must have a being who reveals love relationally.

So love must be defined primarily in terms of being because God Himself is love! "Love" looks like a noun, but it's always a "verb." There can be no love that is fixed on itself or does not make a change. Thus, love belongs to the realm of dynamic existence and cannot simply be defined in our finite language because God Himself is love.

For this reason, the apostle John adds an explanation after he declares, ". . . because God is love." Our finite reason cannot properly understand the "resonance of infinite being" implied in this short sentence. The apostle further explains the love by saying, "In this the love of God was made manifest among us" (v. 9) or "In this is love" (v. 10).

Fallen man cannot comprehend such love in a short, declarative sentence ("God is love!"). So John tells us how that love was actually manifested in a "verb" (v. 9). He also tells us in dynamic detail where that love exists (v. 10).

What does it mean to say that love belongs to God and that God Himself is love? As we see in verses 9-10, God sent His only Son into the world to save us through Him! And it was not that we have loved God, but that God loved us and sent His Son as the propitiation for our sins!

Indeed, there is no greater portrayal of love in the world than that. The apostle's statement is the sum total of all love in the world and the supremacy of love that humans can recognize. It is life itself that makes the dead heart of a sinner beat. I hope that Christian young adults will be able to engrave the content of this supreme love into their beings! And I wish that the emotional intimacy to sprout between the opposite sexes can develop on the basis of this love. We must remember that apart from this love, which forms a special relationship with us, every single moment of our life cannot be meaningful.

Let us relate verses 7-8 to the statement that love should be relational. ". . . for love is from God, and whoever loves has been born of God and knows God. Anyone who does not love does not know God, because God is love." As you can see, "whoever loves has been born of God and knows God." It means that since love belongs to God, the source of love is God. Also, it means that the being of the one who loves cannot be separated from God Himself. Therefore, love must necessarily be relational and accompany the being that causes the relation. It is a blasphemy to try to explain love only conceptually.

Again we get to the second half of verse 8: "because God is love."

This is the conclusion of all verses 7-8. The second half of verse 7 and the first half of verse 8 is, in fact, the reverse of the same content: "whoever loves has been born of God and knows God" (second half of verse 7), and therefore "anyone who does not love does not know God" (first half of verse 8). Taken together, these parts mean that we cannot love God without knowing Him. Why? "Because God is love!"

Now we know exactly the starting point of all love. Only those who know who God is and what He has done for us can speak of love. Because love belongs to God and God Himself is love, all our love from God and knowing God must be based on our relationship with God. I will constantly remind you of that when discussing love from now on. Let's add this sentence and move on to the next one.

"Because God Himself is love,
love must first be defined existentially."

How Can We Define Love? (2)

Now we know that when we define love as being, "Love is God!"[12] But if you just say that and leave it there, this evokes a lot of ques-

---

12) It is simply a reversed expression of the phrase "God is love," not "love is the same with God." C. S. Lewis warns that when the truth that God is love is overturned, and love becomes God, it becomes the demon. C. S. Lewis, *The Four Loves* (New York: Harcourt, Brace and Company, 1960), 17.

tions, especially for young people. It does not mean that the existential definition of love is insufficient, but it means that the definition should be paraphrased to appeal to the five senses of dating people.

We can define love in the "formal aspect" as well as the existential aspect. In this case, the form refers to the components that make up love. But this is by no means referring to the components that make up God. When we say, "Love is God," Love refers to the very existence of God, [13] and that is why this statement is called the existential definition of love.

This time, I would like to argue the definition of love in another dimension. This is the formal aspect of love that I talked about a while ago. Love at this point refers to what is commonly referred to as "conceptual love." Earlier, I asserted that any attempt to explain love only conceptually is an insult to love. That refers to conceptual love which we discuss by excluding the essence and existence of love. I referred to the kind of "love" as blasphemy, which was only conceptually and abstractly discussed, excluding our relationship with God, who is the substance of love.

Psychologists excel at that kind of research. They come up with many theories about love. It is a crucial weak point not to mention the substance of love (the Triune God), but we can gain some insight

13) It does not mean that all attributes of God are love. In this book, the expression "Love is God" is not a concept of systematic theology but rather a kind of rhetoric that describes love as being.

into conceptual love from them. For example, Robert J. Sternberg asserts that the three components of love are "intimacy, passion, and commitment."[14] When these three form an equilateral triangle, he analyzes it as the perfect love. His *Triangular Theory of Love* is still frequently cited in general science.

However, it is necessary to simplify the components of love a bit more and connect it with existential love. The theory of love that ends up as a concept is just a theory. Therefore, the conceptual love discussed here already premises existential love because the forms of conceptual love are based on existential love. From now on, you will gradually understand what this means.

I have been teaching for over ten years on "Dating, Marriage, and the Kingdom of God" in the ministry field. Retrospectively, I had been giving lectures for a much longer time before starting the path of a minister. In every lecture, I ask young people to define what love is in one word. They start pouring out the concepts of love they want to talk about the most. In general, the answer goes like this:

Love is a dedication to him/her.

Love is that I sacrifice my everything for him/her.

Love is to be patient.

Love is to be together to the end.

---

14) See his personal website: http://www.robertjsternberg.com/love (accessed January 8, 2022).

Love is that I give up my time when he/she wants it.

After their answer, I ask another question, "Answer honestly about your symptoms of love." They usually answer like these:

When I fall in love, I miss him/her.

When I fall in love, I remember him/her all day long.

When I love, my heart beats and gets excited.

The more I love, the more I want to have physical contact.

Falling in love is overflowing with happiness.

A closer look reveals something interesting. When asked to say what love is, they almost always refer to love's volitional (will-related) side. The concepts of dedicating, sacrificing, being patient, being together to the end, and giving up are all within the realm of the will. On the other hand, when asked to describe symptoms of love, they almost always refer to the emotional side of love. The concepts of missing, remembering, being excited, wanting physical contact, and overflowing with happiness are all within the realm of emotion.

This phenomenon tells us that conceptual love cannot be defined in one form (or element). Some lecturers said, "Love is a will, not an emotion," but I can't agree with that. In my view, conceptual love involves both will and emotion, and we who experience love are already aware of both. Therefore, it is completely undesirable to teach that love is only a will or claim love only as an emotion.

The forms that make up love include both will and emotion. In other words, the two components that make up conceptual love are "will" and "emotion." Now we have to decide how to understand these two things. If love is neither a will nor an emotion alone, we have to figure out how these two components interact to form whole love. Let's add this sentence and move on to the next one.

"In terms of formality,
love is an operation of the will accompanied by emotion."

 Is Love an Emotion?

This part is also on the continuum of "How Can We Define Love?" Let us recall the last sentence that we have just read. "Love is an operation of the will accompanied by emotion." This is my conclusion when defining love in terms of formality.

It is essential to understand both will and emotion regarding love. How to understand these two factors determines how to love. Some people think of love as a purely emotional component. And some even say that all you need for dating is sensitivity and that dating and love are "a dynamic wave of emotions."[15] They think that love will sprout only when they are attracted by someone emotionally. For example, when they believe they love someone, their heart should pound and be excited.

Such people as them assume him/her to be so. Like themselves, they say that he/she has to have "emotion" of love for themselves, which is evidence that he/she loves them. They believe that all standards of love are in each other's emotional state.

How do people who believe in their emotional state as love usually have a date? They're going to put all of their energy into moving him/her in any way and keeping him/her in an excited, emotional state. To instill the "emotion" (feeling) of love, they pursue endless special events in their daily life. (Shamefully, I'm very poor in this area.) Then one day, when the emotional state towards each other decreases, they become embarrassed of themselves. They think that their love for him/her has diminished or even no longer exists. The opposite is also true. If they don't feel that he/she loves them, they think that he/she doesn't love them anymore.

There was such a couple. After dating for about a month, the brother came and swore they were going to get married. They were filled with the emotion of love. At that moment, I thought that this couple would not go far. Not long after that, the friend came again and said: "Come to think of it, I guess I didn't love her."

Yes! He didn't love her "fully." He had such a "catastrophe" because

---

★

15) 사이몬 후미, 『연애론』, 이소영 옮김 (고양: 봄고양이, 2016), 41.

he put his standard of love on his emotional state. The "emotion" of love disappeared at some point, and he felt embarrassed of himself. According to my analysis of the counseling cases, couples dating for the first time often find themselves in this kind of situation.

So, wouldn't emotional states matter when we love and date? They matter! Naturally, when we fall in passionate love with each other, we are filled with excitement. But we need to know exactly: The "emotion" (or feeling) of love that arises cannot continue in the same state. Even if the emotional state of love is full, there comes the point when the state disappears as time goes by. After that, for some reason, it soars again to a state similar to the beginning. That is, the emotion of love is variable!

Biologists explain the emotion of love as hormone secretion. When a man and woman fall in love, their brain becomes extremely active, releasing several hormones. In general, *dopamine, phenylethylamine, oxytocin,* and *endorphins* are hormones involved in love. That's why these four are called "love hormones." Of these, *oxytocin* is more often referred to as the love hormone because it stimulates a craving for intense physical intimacy.

The secretion of these hormones determines the "emotion" of love during dating. However, the problem is that the hormone secretion state cannot continue to peak. Although there are slight differences among researchers, it is generally said that the hormone secretion decreases rapidly after six months. Interestingly, an actual experiment analyzed the brains of couples in love and produced the same result.[16] Usually, after 18-30 months, the hormonal influence on the same lover almost disappears. From this moment on, the rose-colored glasses come off.

In the past, while conducting couples counseling for a long time, I discovered an interesting fact. The time was concentrated between about six months and one year, in which they started to fight or broke up. Couples dating for the first time showed such a tendency, and I later found out that it almost coincided with the hormonal state that starts when we fall in love. It is easy to find statistics that the average dating period of young people is between six months and one year. We can graph these facts as follows:

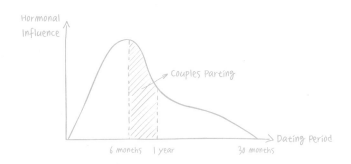

Hormones & Dating Period

★
16) 송용달, 『900일간의 폭풍 사랑』 (서울: 김영사, 2007), 58-64.

Taken together, many couples set the standard for loving each other on their emotional state due to hormone secretion. It is natural to want to feel the "emotion" of passionate love because they are young. But we have to get away from nature to believe that emotion itself is love. Otherwise, the loved one will constantly change according to the secretion of our hormones. While emotion is a required component of love, we must remember that emotion itself is not love.

 Is Love a Will?

While many people believe that love is purely an emotion, surprisingly, many think of love only as a will. The young people in the church show such a tendency rather than those of the world. It may be a case of extreme bias while trying to overcome the harm of believing that love is an emotional state. Or it may be because the body has a weakness that does not secrete love hormones well.

In this section, I would like to examine the case where love is thought of only as a will. How does someone love who believes love is a will? You can get hints from the answers from the actual lectures I mentioned earlier. People usually answered the question "what is love?" in terms of dedication, sacrifice, patience, and willingness to give up. These are all answers that emphasize the volitional (will-related) side. Interestingly, they answered the symptoms of love: missing, remembering, excited, wanting physical contact, and overflowing with happiness. These are all answers related to love's emotional side.

As previously argued, both of these sides are included in conceptual love. In particular, young Christian people consider love as a volitional side because they are usually exposed to such content. 1 Corinthians 13, which is called the "Love Chapter," emphasizes love's volitional side very much.

The volitional side of love is very prominent, but we must not think of love as only a will. Like me in the past, the more emotionally blunt and more rational they are, the stronger their tendency to think of love as a will. They try to taboo the emotional turbulence when young men and women fall in love. One of the reasons for thinking like that is the atmosphere in the church where the "emotion" of love is considered a sin. But the emotion naturally comes out between lovers when dating.

Of course, it seems that the atmosphere has changed a lot these days. Many churches offer high-quality education in this area by opening dating courses for middle and high school students and young adults. Although those are often limited to a developmental psychological diagnosis, dealing with the natural emotions of men and women in the image of God is very positive.

However, it was socially taboo to express emotions between the opposite sexes in a generation older than me. In particular, there was an atmosphere of sacrilege in the church, which is the testimony I heard directly from my mother-in-law, a senior in the faith. Under these circumstances, Christians are not good at analyzing and expressing the "emotions" of love. Even some people who are much younger than I often criticize my dating lectures as impure.

For one reason or another, many people think that love is only a will. The way they love is somewhat artificial and obsessive. Rather than his/her emotion and mind, the cause and purpose of dating are unwittingly first and foremost. That is, we should not be swayed by mere emotions when it comes to dating and marriage. They try to understand love only as dedication, patience, continuing sacrifice, and giving up on what is theirs. They don't really care about each other's emotions and minds in the process. In adolescence, this tendency is especially seen in men rather than women.

When I was in college, I read *The Art of Loving* by Erich Fromm (1900-1980), a social psychologist. I have been interested in serious dating and love since my teenage years, so I could feel the novelty throughout reading his book. It was like cold water in summer to me, who tabooed emotional turbulence during dating. Hormonal emotion was not crucial in defining and analyzing love. Actually, he said, "To love somebody is not just a strong feeling."[17]

His way of portraying love as *an art* was marvelous to me at that time. Like acquiring "skills" in music, painting, or architecture, love

17) Erich Fromm, *The Art of Loving*, 56.

should be approached as a skill, and it is an approach that sounds a warning to modern people who want to reckon love as a strong emotion.

I fully sympathize with Fromm's intentions, but it's hard to accept his views fully. This is because the turbulent emotional state of love has a profound effect on actual dating or marriage. We should not blindly proclaim that love is a volitional skill, but we should make a biblical diagnosis and suggest alternatives to such a part. We need to give a balanced perspective to those who taboo the emotion of love and believe love is the same as a will.

Think about it: What would happen if lovers had no emotional response to the fact that they loved, and treated each other only with a skill? Do you want to date or have a married life with thorough self-control and volitional skills without reacting "volitionally" to such intense emotions? From my point of view, who is gradually becoming an "emotional man," it seems terrifying to think about it.

 ## Love, the Will Accompanied by Emotion

Now we should combine the will and emotion of love. As I've mentioned several times, from a formal (or functional) standpoint, love is an operation of the will accompanied by emotion. There was a process that led to this conclusion. It is because of my firm principle that love must first be defined as being, and of my belief that "existential love" should be expressed as "conceptual love." In other words, these two aspects of love belong to different realms, but those must be expressed holistically and not separated from each other.

Since I was in college, I had been seriously thinking about how to understand the relationship between will and emotion in love. Then one day, a theological principle flashed through my mind. The relationship between faith and works (obedience) in salvation came into my mind. As I pondered, I realized that this theological principle is a clue that links existential and conceptual love and provides a holistic explanation.

I will mention it again as a reminder. *Existential love* means that the Triune God Himself is love. Love is not a fixed noun but being itself and a "verb" causing differences. In this context, I freely accept Fromm's statement that "love is an activity, not a passive affect."[18] And *conceptual love* refers to love's components (will and emotion) that premise existential love. It is an area that deals with love conceptually, either formally or functionally.

Existential love and conceptual love can never be separated. Why? Because, in dealing with any concept, it is impossible to think apart from the existence of God for even a moment. All daily life and concepts come to us as "living meaning" only when directed toward the Triune God. To put it in Christology, our redeemed reason and eyes must see and interpret all phenomena and concepts through the lens of the cross.

So I try to correspond the "will and emotion" of love to the relationship between "faith and works" of salvation. As mentioned earlier, the Bible is often likening our relationship with God to that of a husband and wife (or groom and bride) because the marriage instituted by God ultimately aims for the mystical union of Christ and the church. Then it is concluded that we can correspond the essence (salvation) of existential love to the components (will and emotion) of conceptual love. Each represents the following:

1. The essence of existential love is that God granted us salvation, and we have to express salvation as faith and works.
2. The components of conceptual love appear between husband and wife, who manifest the mystical union.

Let's break it down in a diagram to make it easier to understand.

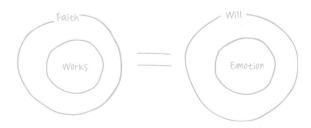

Existential Love vs. Conceptual Love[19]

As you can see from the diagram, faith corresponds to will, and works correspond to emotion. There is a reason I set up this way. It's because just as our salvation is based on faith, so our love is based on will.

The fundamental attribute of love is "will." Above all, the Bible text testifies to it. Please take a look at 1 Corinthians 13:4-7 mentioned earlier.

Love is patient and kind; love does not envy or boast; it is not arrogant or rude. It does not insist on its own way; it is not irritable or resentful; it does not rejoice at wrongdoing, but rejoices with the truth. Love bears all things, believes all things, hopes all things, endures all things.

These are the statements of the apostle Paul, which are the so-called *Love Chapter.* Read carefully the way the apostle describes love. All in all, he emphasizes the volitional (will-related) aspect of love. Interestingly, it starts with "being patient" and ends with "enduring." So love is patient and endures from beginning to end.

Paul inserts the Love Chapter because there is a context that has to do with the abuse of gifts. Chapters 12 and 14 are the so-called *Gift Chapters,* and Chapter 13 is unexpectedly inserted between them.

*

19) The correct name is "The Essence of Existential Love vs. The Components of Conceptual Love."

Considering Paul's temperament accustomed to sophisticated logic, it is quite intentional. It is a structure that emphasizes the necessity of loving saints when using supernatural gifts such as tongues and prophecy. That is why it highlights the volitional aspect of "patient and enduring" love for the sake of community order and virtue.

Despite this context, the text simultaneously testifies to the universal nature of love. It also alludes to the depiction of Christ as love itself.[20] Thus, all kinds of love can be discussed based on the Love Chapter. Love in dating and marriage differs from other types of love only in that it involves an exclusive relationship. Still, the universal nature of love applies to all kinds of love. For this reason, I claim that the Bible is the supreme guide to the study of love.

After all, love is fundamentally rooted in the will. The emotion of love must flow from this "will." This is the same principle in soteriology that our works (obedience) must be derived from faith. As you can see from the diagram, our faith includes works, and love's will embraces emotions. Expressing this emotional will toward the opposite sex is the beginning of love. Therefore, love is an operation of the will accompanied by emotion.

We need to break free from the dichotomy of separating will and emotion in love. Just as when we say that salvation comes only through faith, this faith premises works. When we say love is a will,

---

★

20) 리고니어 미니스트리, 『개혁주의 스터디 바이블』, 김진운 외 옮김 (서울: 부흥과개혁사, 2017), 2048.

we must understand that the will already premises emotion. And we must also remember that having a will to love does not always involve emotions, just as having a saving faith does not always involve works.

By reversing this principle, we can gain great insight. Just as morally good works do not necessarily imply that a person has the saving "faith," having special emotions for someone does not necessarily imply that he/she has the "will" to love! Why? Because, just as the criterion for being saved is not works, the criterion for loving is not based on emotions. I want you to think about how you love during dating.

Dating Like Artificial Flowers

More and more young people seem to date like artificial flowers. Even though there is no vitality in dating, they want to maintain their unchanging beauty. The vitality, in this case, is the will of love. They are accustomed to dating where they look at each other, not to love looking together in the same direction. We, fallen humans, are finite by nature, so if we look at and expect each other, we cannot have the vitality of love. We spend a short dating mistaking sexual arousal for its vitality.

Even though there are no roots buried in the ground or the roots are decaying, young people are very focused on the branches and fruits visible above the ground. Many young couples continue to show each other their beauty but increasingly feel their inner emptiness. Even if they once had a stormy love, the stillness of silence swallows up their love after some time.

Now we need to stop dating like artificial flowers and start loving like natural flowers. They sometimes wither but can always retain their original beauty with the right environment and nutrients. Why? Because they are living things with deep roots in the ground.

So I want to encourage young people. I hope you don't like "consistent" romance in dating too much! Does he/she show you only the beautiful and wonderful side unchangingly? If so, please try it once in a while. He/she may be dating like artificial flowers, which maintain a consistent beauty on the outside, but no life in him/her.

The opposite is also true. Are you putting all your energies into showing him/her your unchanging beauty? Unless it's a natural reaction from the will of love, it's just a kind of compulsion to try to be good at dating. It may be a disproof of your fear that his/her attraction to you will disappear.

Now we need to restore the vitality of love. We should remember that love's emotion can change, but love's will can be unchanging once the couple "take root" in one direction. We should be more concerned with the operation of the much unchanging "will" than with the variable emotional states. I hope you have peace of mind to accept his/her "inconsistency" during dating naturally.

Then there remains a thing to be done in earnest. We should think seriously about how to root the will of love. This will is the first step towards the "relative substance" which is marriage. It is a step towards a marriage that bears witness to the mystical union (ultimate substance) of Christ and the church. At this point, Christian dating must be different from the world's dating. So, what should we do so that the will to love may take root during dating?

This Is What Sustains Love!

Again, love is an operation of the will accompanied by emotion. It is easy to start dating by being drawn to the emotion of love, but it must take "will" to continue dating after the emotion has disappeared. Young men and women don't feel burdened when dating because their hormones are extremely active. In this case, stormy love is possible. In the early stages of dating, it is simply a series of voluntary attractions.

In this way, love hormones provide a burst of power for couples to keep their relationship going. However, lovers begin to feel that their love is cooling off over time. When the love cools down, it means that the "emotion" towards each other cools down as the hormone secretion decreases. From this moment on, another component of love must come into play. Have you already noticed that I keep emphasizing "will" as one of the two components of love?

The importance of the will in love is also emphasized in general studies, and doctors as well as psychologists say the same. I will introduce the words of Professor Marzetti of the Department of Psychiatry, University of Pisa in Italy. She said:

Even without hormones, love will not disappear as long as there is a human will. We often forget the importance of a will, but we must not forget that it takes a lot of hard efforts to love a person fully. [21]

This paragraph is the word of an expert who studied 12 couples in love. She emphasizes that the absence of hormone secretion does not mean that love disappears because humans have a "will." In other words, when the hormonal influence dissipates and the rose-colored glasses come off, what lovers need is the will of love from then on.

While we emphasize the will in love, we may ask a question at some point. The question is, "Why should I have a will to love this person?" Actually, when I give lectures to young people, I am often asked the question. While I keep emphasizing that love is an operation of the will accompanied by emotion, they are often curious about what criteria we should operate the will of love.

This question is inevitable. They don't even think about it when they're caught up in the "emotion" of a stormy love. They were all in a state of sexual arousal, drawn to each other with no time to think. Then as the rose-

---

★
21) 송웅달, 『900일간의 폭풍 사랑』, 68.

colored glasses come off, everyone is bound to ask such a question. Some people think about the will of love from the beginning, but even those who don't will inevitably ask such questions when their emotions start to disappear. However, it is simply expressed differently by saying, "Why do I date this person?"

Now is the time to step out of looking at each other. As I quoted previously, love is looking together in the same direction. This "same direction" sustains the love of Christian couples. Couples of the world think they are looking in the same direction, but there is no reality. The same direction they are talking about is just an abstract concept or a vague idea that is ultimately decided by each other. Therefore, they only comfort each other by saying, "The small convictions of every moment gather to support our love."[22] The basis for that conviction is the inner psychological state they create.

But Christian young adults must be different. We have a clear basis for our conviction, and there is a "same direction" for all lovers to look in. It is also the "same direction" with a distinct reality. It is the ultimate goal for all Christians as well as loved ones to walk towards. I outlined it initially, but we'll get to it in the next chapter.

---

22) 최유수, 『사랑의 목격』 (서울: 허밍버드, 2020), 88.

1. Please freely express the definition of love you usually think of.

2. Explain in your own language that love must be relational, especially in relation to the gospel we believe in.

3. Have you ever fallen in a stormy love? Candidly share how your emotional state or body reacted toward him/her at that time.

4. Among the will and emotion of love, which one is the primary way you love? If you are dating, to which side is your current state closer?

5. Explain the phrase "love is an operation of the will accompanied by emotion" by comparing it to the relationship between faith and works.

Chapter 3.

Biblical Principles for Dating

Previously, I mentioned "everyday life's direction." It is the glorious God's kingdom that is currently in progress and will be consummated in the future, which is directly related to all of our daily lives. The direction is His kingdom that will change into "a new heaven and a new earth" (Rev. 21:1), which cannot be compared with this world in its present state. This kingdom of God and all the blessings promised in it are the reality of the "same direction" we should look at.

Christian couples must first be able to engrave this reality into their souls. It is the ultimate reality and basis for operating the will of love. After the stormy love's emotion withers, you begin to look outside for reasons to support your love from then on. In those days filled with burning emotions, you look inside and mistakenly believe that "our love will last forever." That's because you are caught up in the turbulence of emotions that no one can shake. It would be a state in which emotion overwhelms reason.

Then when the love hormone disappears, the reason is restored, and you begin to feel sane. At this point, two reactions occur. It's either a reaction that you don't love him/her anymore or a reaction that requires you to find a cause for loving him/her other than your emotional state. I want you to think for yourself which one you relate to.

Now the reason that can operate the will of love has been restored. At this time, unlike those in the world, we must put the root of the will "in the same direction." It is the external force that sustains the will of love. Also, it is the ultimate reality that all Christians must look forward to and God's kingdom that will be consummated in the future. In other words, the same direction lovers must look at is "God's vision."

So, what do you think "vision" is? One of the dictionary definitions of vision is "something that you imagine: a picture that you see in your mind,"[23] often meaning a personal dream, goal, or plan. However, the vision in the Bible goes beyond the individual level and points to God's dream and plan. The word *vision* comes from the Latin word *videre,* which means "to see."[24] It has the same meaning as the Greek verb *horaō* (ὁράω).[25] Revelation 7:9-12 contains this word and God's vision.

[9]After this I looked, and behold, a great multitude that no one could number, from every nation, from all tribes and peoples and languages, standing before the throne and before the Lamb, clothed in white robes, with palm branches in their hands, [10]and crying out with a loud voice, "Salvation belongs to our God who sits on the throne, and to the Lamb!" [11]And all the angels were standing around the

23) See this website: https://www.merriam-webster.com/dictionary/vision (accessed January 8, 2022).

24) Catherine Soanes and Angus Stevenson, eds., "vision," in *Concise Oxford English Dictionary* (Oxford: Oxford University Press, 2004).

25) William Arndt, Frederick W. Danker, and Walter Bauer, *A Greek-English Lexicon of the New Testament and Other Early Christian Literature* (Chicago: University of Chicago Press, 2000), 279.

throne and around the elders and the four living creatures, and they fell on their faces before the throne and worshiped God, [12]saying, "Amen! Blessing and glory and wisdom and thanksgiving and honor and power and might be to our God forever and ever! Amen."

The Greek word for "looked" in verse 9 has the same meaning as the English word for vision.[26] This passage is about the scene that the Lord showed the apostle John, and he is looking at it. So the vision is that we see what the Lord is showing us.

What is the apostle looking at? He is looking at the final consummation of the kingdom of God. "A great multitude that no one could number," that is, all the saints who believe in the Lamb Jesus, are crying out loudly the "salvation" of God, which angels will never know. Because angels have never experienced salvation, they cannot enjoy the supreme thrill like us. God dreams of the day when we will praise Him with the angels forever. This is the reality of the "same direction" and God's vision.

Because vision is that we see what God is showing us, God's vision is our vision. We should not think of our short-term goals and plans as if they were the ultimate vision. The content of the text that God showed the apostle must be the ultimate vision for all of us!

---

26) To add, the Greek verb ὁράω for "looked" is translated *videre* in the Latin text, and from this Latin verb, the word *vision* comes from.

Are you truly dreaming of the day when "a new heaven and a new earth" will come and the whole world will be filled with the glory and presence of God? Are you really looking forward to the day when we will praise the Triune God forever and ever in His kingdom where there will be no more sin, sorrow, suffering, and death with all who believe in Christ? Do you indeed long for the hand of God who will wipe away all our tears? Are you actually living conscious of "the world to come" in which the mystical union of Christ and the church will be fully enjoyed?

I am really looking forward to that day coming soon. I earnestly hope that the Lord will come soon and restore this world to a perfect state, where there will no longer be famine, calamity, and pandemics. We must not mistake our departure from this sin-polluted world for final salvation! That is, we should not think of our souls as if living forever in the "paradise" in which we reside temporarily. In this world that will be transformed into "a new heaven and a new earth," the day will come, and we will spend eternity with God in the glorious resurrection body. This is our final salvation and the completion of God's kingdom.

Therefore, our everyday life is converging towards that day. Even dating and marriage are by no means an exception. Especially couples in love should keep that in mind. Love isn't looking at each other but is looking together "in the same direction." When the emotion of love is extinguished, we should fix the will of love in that direction. If you can, you should be able to pour overflowing energy "in the same direction," even when you're in a stormy love.

 ## How Do I Build My Will? (1)

On what can we root the will of love in dating? This is a question that has already been asked, and now it's time to answer it. In the preceding section, I have described the reality that every Christian must ultimately look at. Couples unmarried or married are no exception to that.

So, on what basis should couples build the "will" of love, which is essential for marriage? Now we need to remember the "mission" that God has given us. We must keep in mind that we are not just beings who enjoy each other's love but that we are His creatures fulfilling a mission. In conclusion, God's vision is the external basis for supporting the will of love. And each other's mission is the inner criterion for operating the will of love.

Let me explain a bit more about what I mean. The will of love refers to the desire to love the opposite sex for our ultimate vision (God's vision). That is to say, it means the will itself to want to date even if the loved one has not been decided yet. Of course, the reality is that many people want to meet him/her attracted to them regardless of God's vision. Correcting that is one of the purposes of this book.

There comes a time when young people who have started dating have to decide whether to marry or not. At that time, they seriously ponder on what basis they should operate the will of love. Its standard should be each other's "mission." This mission is the response that takes place within us to the drawing of the Holy Spirit. So a mission is an inner criterion by which the will of love operates.

Many Christian couples are mistaken. The fact that they love each other can make their married life happy. Of course, as long as the love hormone lasts, the happiness they say may be true. But, as we have argued before, there is necessarily a point in time when the burning emotion of love is extinguished, no matter how stormy it is. If the burning condition lasts a lifetime, the married couple cannot live normally. If you don't know what I mean, think of a couple falling in love and crazy about each other.

We, creatures, can be happy ultimately because we know God. I wish you will take to heart the confession of St. Augustine (354-430), who said, ". . . happy whoso knoweth Thee, . . . but for Thee only."[27] God gives couples a temporary taste of burning love so that they can realize that God loves them so passionately. Our finite body cannot sustain the stormy emotions of love, so He withdraws those for the sake of our health and life.

27) St. Augustine Bishop of Hippo, *The Confessions of St. Augustine*, V.iv, trans. E. B. Pusey (Oak Harbor, WA: Logos Research Systems, Inc., 1996).

Now couples must let go of the idea that burning love makes a happy marriage! Married as well as unmarried couples can enjoy true happiness when they are captivated by God's vision and armed with the sense of mission He has given them. Do you know what the primary purpose of man is? "To glorify God, and to enjoy Him forever."[28] We must remember that lovers can enjoy true purpose and happiness when they exalt God and enjoy Him.

God gave the "mission" as the principle for marriage. Genesis 2 introduces humankind's first dating and marriage. God caused a deep sleep to fall upon Adam, took one of his ribs, made a woman, and brought her to Adam. Every time I imagine this scene, I keep thinking of the bride's father holding his daughter's hand as they enter the wedding hall. It can be interpreted to mean that the first wedding ceremony of humankind is being reproduced even today.

Anyway, what was Adam doing before the first dating and marriage took place? Was he vaguely lonely because he looked at other animals and didn't have a mate for him? Before that, God "led" Adam and placed him in the Garden of Eden to work and keep it (Gen. 2:15). In response to God's leading, Adam was carrying out the "mission" of cultivating and protecting the Garden of Eden diligently.

In this context, humankind's first dating and marriage took place. Therefore, dating and marriage were directly related to the mission

★

28) WSC, Q. 1. What is the chief end of man? A. Man's chief end is to glorify God, and to enjoy him forever.

82

God gave us from the beginning. We all have a God-given mission. But some people just don't recognize it.

God calls sinners to a state of salvation[29] and necessarily gives them a mission to contribute to the fulfillment of God's vision. At this point, calling us to a mission is referred to as a "missional calling." Those who are called to a state of salvation (i.e., effectual calling) are also called to a mission to fulfill God's vision. These two aspects of the calling need to be distinct, but those can never be separated.

The risen Lord, who came as a light on the way to Damascus, called the persecutor Saul (Paul) and gave him the mission of an evangelist to the nations through Ananias (Acts 9:15-16). Of course, Paul had a unique experiential characteristic. Still, the Lord's principle of calling us to a state of salvation and a mission is the same for all. Actually, the apostle Paul connects God's calling and mission throughout his epistles.[30]

In the context of God's absolute sovereignty, a mission is decided for each of us (passive side). However, in terms of our response to His leading, we must actively pioneer that mission (active side). Please remember that God "led" Adam into the Garden of Eden, but Adam "actively" carried out the mission of working and keeping it. It is an

---

29) In doctrinal terms, it is called an "effectual calling." It is well described in the Westminster Short Catechism, Q. 31. What is effectual calling? A. Effectual calling is the work of God's Spirit, whereby, convincing us of our sin and misery, enlightening our minds in the knowledge of Christ, and renewing our wills, he does persuade and enable us to embrace Jesus Christ, freely offered to us in the gospel.
30) 김세윤, 『칭의와 성화』 (서울: 두란노, 2013), 224.

insult to His sovereignty to say that God has not given me a mission, so I have no choice but to live the way I live. If we trust in God's absolute sovereignty, we can actively and enterprisingly pioneer and discover our mission while firmly relying on His guidance even at the moment we respond. A more in-depth discussion seems beyond the scope of this book, so I'll cover it in another book later.

God's vision, His calling, and our mission are inseparable. Even the daily routines (including dating and marriage) and plans for realizing the mission cannot be considered in isolation. Why? Because our very existence is related to the fulfillment of God's vision. Let's break it down in a diagram to make it easier to understand.

As you can see, everyday life and plans eventually converge to God's vision. In addition, our daily life and plans act as factors for realizing our mission. God's calling to lead us to this mission also acts as

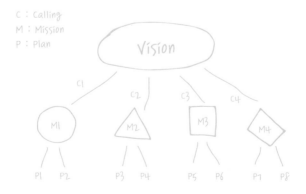

Vision vs. Calling vs. Mission

a providence. And all of these things come together and contribute to the fulfillment of God's vision.

Therefore, Christian couples should be conscious of God's vision, calling, and mission while enjoying burning love. In particular, you must go through the process of confirming and coordinating each other's missions for marriage. Are you convinced that marriage contributes to the fulfillment of God's vision and testifies to the mystical union of Christ and the church? Then you do not decide whether to marry simply because of loving him/her. You are seriously contemplating how much you will dedicate yourself to completing God's kingdom (i.e., world evangelization) by marrying him/her. Also, you are considering how effectively you will unfold your mission by coordinating it in one direction. Usually, we realize that later after we get married, but heavenly blessings will come upon couples who realize this principle and prepare for it before marriage.

 ## How Do I Build My Will? (2)

Let's be more specific. If the "mission" of each other should be the standard when rooting the will of love, how can we apply the principle in real situations? The terms used may be a bit unfamiliar, but they are simpler than you think.

In the past, I participated in Mission Korea.[31] Among the questions raised there, there was a question related to dating, and it was a question about a couple in love. The brother had the mission of missionary work overseas and was preparing diligently. At the same time, the sister considered domestic missionary work as her mission.

However, the problem was that their convictions about each mission did not waver. It seems that someone asked a question in a lecture on what to do in this case. The lecturer did not respond properly, so a sister carefully brought out her words during our group meeting. However, no one was speaking, so I started to answer. Because I was married at that time and had been seriously thinking about dating since my teenage years, I answered confidently according to the principles in this book.

What should the couple do if their missions are never shaken? Still, what should they do if their hearts are full of love for each other? So if the desire to marry continues, what decision should they make?

First of all, these concerns are already disproving that love alone cannot make a marriage decision. Because if the only thing needed for marriage is love, then there can be no such conflict. This couple struggles because they are full of love for each other, but both could't

---

31) Mission Korea Conference began in 1988, the 100th anniversary of the SVM (Student Volunteer Movement) that took place in the United States in 1888, with the dedication of the JOY Mission, which dreamed of mobilizing young Korean college students to missions. The conference is held every two years in early August and is open to young Christian college students from all over the country. For more details, see this website: http://missionkorea.org/대회/ (accessed January 8, 2022).

back down their own missions. If they came for counseling with the case, what advice would be the wisest?

I divided my answers into three cases. First, I asked them to check whether they were absolutely sure of their missions. Suppose the brother can never give up missionary work abroad and the sister can never give up domestic missionary work. In that case, it is no longer possible to root the will of love. In other words, the two have no choice but to break up. It's not that they break up because they don't love. Instead, because they love each other, they break up with respect for each other's mission.

Next, I asked them to consider whether they could coordinate the direction of their missions on one side. No matter how confident they are with their missions, these cannot have absolute authority like the Bible. They need to know how to let go of their firm thoughts sometimes. Because you love him/her, you give up your mission and happily conform to his/her mission. Then you should be sure that his/her mission is yours.

Finally, I asked them to think about whether they could align the direction of their missions by talking to each other. It is to readjust the brother's missionary work overseas considering the sister's domestic missionary work on one side. For example, they can consider domestic ministry for foreign residents or overseas ministry in connection with domestic missionary work. It does not mean that they give up and compromise on each mission. Rather, it happens naturally through the providence of God, who understands the hearts of the couple.

In any case, the second and third cases are situations in which the will of love takes root. They are cases of starting a full-fledged step towards marriage to fulfill God's vision.[32] Here's a principle we can find out: Dating is the process of confirming and coordinating each other's missions while having a stormy love. So, the love of a couple does not have any meaning in love itself but has true meaning when they sincerely respond to the shared mission that God is leading.

Here are suggestions when building the will of love for marriage, considering each other's missions. First, the mission you are convinced of should not be the criterion for "judging" him/her. That is, you must not instrumentalize the other for your mission. We must not approach in such a way that we have to keep arguing whether he/she fits our "great" mission and find a match worthy of it. This attitude itself directly violates love's attributes. People who are too obsessed with their sense of mission often show such a rigid attitude.

Second, you need to know that even if you have not yet discovered your mission, it can be created through him/her during the dating. The opposite is also true. God can use the dating process as a way to call you into a mission. Therefore, there should be no case of being diffident or condemned for not discovering the mission. Dating is not

★

32) It refers to the completion of the kingdom of God (i.e., world evangelization), and it means to enjoy the mystical union of Christ and the church substantially.

A Theology of Dating

yet as perfect love as marriage, but you should refrain from loving the other based on his/her conditions from the beginning.

Third, you must not make the mistake of equating a mission with a job. I often see that many people think of their mission based on the job. Job is the means to actualize the mission, not the mission itself. Our mission is to serve the field of life, ruled by the Lord, with the gospel by using our job as a means. Therefore, just because the jobs are the same or different, this should not be a standard to build the will of love. Even if a couple has the same kind of job, their dating or marriage can be far from the mission. Even if they have different jobs, they can go together for dating and marriage as "missionaries" (i.e., mission-doers).

In summary, each other's mission is the criterion for building the will of love for marriage. Christian young adults should know that love alone is not the only way to marry. Although love is a necessary factor in marriage, it is not a necessary and sufficient condition. I wish that more and more couples can confirm and coordinate each other's missions for the sake of God's kingdom while having a burning love.

 ## A Dating Story Related to Mission

Due to the characteristics of this book, it would be good to introduce my episode. I am a pastor with 15 years of marriage.[33] When I was in middle school, I felt being called to be a pastor and missionary at a church retreat. Since then, I prepared for the path of a minister. But I forsook the Lord's calling for a while during my military service. Still, I experienced His dramatic grace and obeyed again.

After being discharged from the military, I returned to college. I was introduced to my current wife while concentrating on my studies. Since I was already preparing for the path of a minister, I told the truth from the beginning. I said, "If you fall in love with me and are married, you might become a pastor's wife." Moreover, I honestly shared my troubled family circumstances (domestic violence, divorced family).

Surprisingly, unlike any sisters I had met before, she said she would just start "cool" dating. As I said previously, I had a bit of eccentric dating. We met at a cafe to study the English Bible together and even had a prayer meeting in my share house. In other people's eyes, she seemed much bored because of me at that time. However, according to her confession, she really enjoyed the grace of being filled with the Holy Spirit. If you don't believe it, ask her yourself.

While dating her, I went to the cinema for the first time in my life. I was utterly ignorant of even the styles and fashions that women like. I was shy and had almost no dating sense. Anyone could see that I was treating women in a no-nonsense way. Even thinking about it now, it

---

★

33) Now I have been married for 17 years while writing this English manuscript.

feels like a miracle that I dated her and got married.

Before being married, we had a serious conversation about our mission. I said, "I'm already preparing for the path of a minister. So I was just wondering if you have a mission that you are sure God has given." She said thoughtfully, "I have been praying for missions in the Philippines. Whenever I cherish the Philippines and pray for them, I often cry because of souls there."

I started to feel sorry to hear her answer. I majored in English at that time but had no foreign experience, so I never thought about missionary work overseas. On the last day of the church retreat in my mid-10s, I just walked out to the front of the stage when the worship leader told us, saying, "Come up here, if you want to devote yourselves as a pastor and missionary." Since my teenage years, I had a vague idea of becoming a pastor or a missionary. Therefore, even if she married me, she might not fulfill her mission in the Philippines.

Thankfully, she decided to give up her mission because of me. I did not force her, but she gladly chose to participate in my mission. We fall into the second type introduced earlier. Because we loved each other, it is a case in which we coordinated our missions to one side.

But something amazing happened. Now, 15 years have passed since then, and my family is preparing for missions in the Philippines. We are preparing for the ministry of teaching seminary students in Bohol, Philippines. Originally, I served as an intensive lecture for one week of seminary students in Mongolia every year. Then last year,

I visited the Philippines for the first time. I spent half of it on family summer vacation and half as a seminary partner ministry. While teaching seminarians, we deeply shared the gospel fellowship with the missionary couple.

After returning to Korea, my wife and I started to long for the Philippines. One day, she said, "Let's go!" I doubted my ears. When I took my family to Mongolia for the first time, she had a very trying experience. So I thought that she would never go to a mission field again. But now, with her great determination, my family is currently preparing for missions to the Philippines.[34]

As I was writing the manuscript for this book, I suddenly remembered the mission she shared during our dating before marriage. I discovered the amazing providence that God did not forget the mission buried in my heart and fulfilled it in due time. I thought her mission was going to end because of me, but God was calling me a pastor and "missionary" and fulfilling her mission at the same time.

In this way, God unfolds the mission that couples cherish and pray for during dating. He is still looking for couples obsessed with the sense of mission given by Him while they are looking forward to the completion of His kingdom. However, you don't have to spend your dating like me in a no-nonsense way. A missionary (a mission-doer)

---

34) We could not enter the Philippines due to the coronavirus pandemic. Two years later, my family is currently living a missionary life in Korea. I teach seminary students of the Philippines and Mongolia online.

couple is enough, who enjoys a stormy love while thinking of God's vision and obeying His calling.

Is It Appointed? Is It My Choice? (1)

There is a question I get asked frequently during couples counseling. They want to know whether or not he/she is the mate God has appointed. They often say, "I want to marry, but I'm wondering if it is God's will to marry this person." How should we answer this question?

I would rather ask myself. Is such a question really Scripturally valid? First of all, they are making two false premises without their knowledge. One is the fatalistic idea that God has already appointed a "specific" mate for me, and the other is the misapplication of the matter of personal choice as God's will. It is an idea and concept that are commonly used casually. So many believers, including myself at one time, naturally accepted such a premise.

Jesus said, "What therefore God has joined together, let not man separate" (Matt. 19:6b; Mark 10:9). The Greek verb *suzeugnumi* (συ-ζεύγνυμι) for "to join together" literally means "to yoke together."[35]

35) William Arndt, et al., *A Greek-English Lexicon of the New Testament and Other Early Christian Literature*, 954.

So this verse says that God now yokes both of them simultaneously, making them inseparable partners for each other's needs and responsibilities.[36]

Therefore, we should not mistakenly believe that God appointed my spouse in advance. Jesus's word means that God will change the relationship between the two previously single into a married relationship.[37] Simply put, marriage is not formed when we get married, but is formed because God approves our marriage. In this context, we should understand the word "God has joined together."

In conclusion, God is not the one who has appointed a certain mate for you and asks you to find out him/her.[38] However, we can cautiously express that He foresees whom I will meet in the context of God's absolute sovereignty and infallible foreknowledge. Even in that case, we must thoroughly reject any intention to attribute our responsibility to God.

The fatalistic idea that God has appointed a specific mate directly opposes our free will. This idea is based on the premise that "only one way is the best for me." In other words, the idea is that the best mate prepared for me is a "specific person." But for us, the best way is not just one, but manifests as many possibilities according to our free will,

★

36) John Nolland, *The Gospel of Matthew: A Commentary on the Greek Text,* NIGTC (Grand Rapids, MI: W.B. Eerdmans, 2005), 773.

37) Lane T. Dennis, et al., eds., *ESV Study Bible* (Wheaton, Illinois: Crossway, 2008), 1860.

38) It is usually thought that the prophet Hosea is such a case, but in reality, it is not. God did not command him to marry Gomer. But He said, "Go, take to yourself a wife of whoredom" (Hos. 1:2).

only on the premise that it should not lead to the realm of sin.

After God created man and gave him a mission ("to work and keep"), He spoke exactly such a word (Gen. 2:15-17):

> [15]The LORD God took the man and put him in the garden of Eden to work it and keep it. [16]And the LORD God commanded the man, saying, "You may surely eat of every tree of the garden, [17]but of the tree of the knowledge of good and evil you shall not eat, for in the day that you eat of it you shall surely die."

There is only one thing God forbids man. Eating the fruit of the tree of the knowledge of good and evil is forbidden because it is a terrible sin that cuts off our relationship with God. Except for going into the realm of sin, He says, "You may surely eat." In other words, it means, "Make your choices with the free will that you have, but do not commit a sin against me."

Yet, rather than focusing on the single thing God forbids, we usually focus on the single thing that we think God best requires. "The single best thing that God requires" is a thought created by ourselves, not God. Instead, God wants us to be free and to challenge many possibilities. If we do not go into the realm of sin, He respects our choices and guides the results in the best direction, even if the results of our choice appear clumsy.

The fear of failure is rooted in the thought that God appointed a specific mate for me. That is, my life may fail if I marry a mate whom God does not want me to marry. However, this kind of thinking stems from a misunderstanding of God's disposition. Do you think that the God of love has given us one of the best options, and if we don't find it, He troubles us? I don't believe in such a "God!" From parents' point of view, they want their children to make their own choices freely, and they want to help them lead to the best result of their choices.

Then will the God of love treat us fatalistically? By no means! Are you struggling with the thought during dating, "Is this person really the destined mate God has appointed?" I hope you will soon put aside such worries and choose freely by "seriously considering" each other's missions! It's up to your choice to marry him/her or not. God will respect your choice and guide you to the best no matter what the results of your choices happen.

 ## Is It Appointed? Is It My Choice? (2)

Nevertheless, the question might remain in your mind, whether there is God's will for the choice problem. Now we need to establish the use of the term biblically. We should also pay close attention to how the word "will" of God is used in the Bible. The will of God in the Bible has nothing to do with personal choice. As I have stated in my other book, the will of God has to do with the issue of our salvation and especially the universality of our life of faith.[39]

That is to say, it is God's will that everyone who sees and believes in the Son of God has eternal life (John 6:40), and it is God's will that Jesus gave Himself to save us (Gal. 1:4). Also, it is God's will for us to be holy (1 Thess. 4:3), and it is God's will for us always to rejoice, pray, and give thanks in everything (1 Thess. 5:16-18). Many other Bible verses contain the "will" of God, and from what I've analyzed, those are all in the same context.

As you can see, God's will is not a matter of personal choice. God's will is clearly revealed in the written word of the Bible. His will is the intention that He predestines, applies, and requires from us necessarily. It is not a matter of personal choice whether we gain eternal life and be saved. And it is not our choice to be holy and always rejoice, pray, and give thanks. It is God's good intention that we must obey. That is, we have no choice as to the will of God.

Then how should we express the often misused "will of God?" It should be expressed as God's "guidance" or "providence" (i.e., preservation and rule). It is a realm of free will where we can freely choose in prayer, as long as we don't run into the realm of sin. As we have argued earlier, the best paths for us are variously open in this area. That is why you shouldn't think that the best mate you can marry is

39) 권율, 『올인원 주기도문』 (서울: 세움북스, 2018), 64.

the "appointed person" by God in advance. No matter who you marry depends on your choices, he/she can be the best mate for you.

At this point, we must be precise: "I" chose him/her by relying on God's guidance or providence. God's guidance at this time is not a check that guarantees my choice itself was perfect. Instead, it is a confession of faith that my free choice is within God's sovereignty. In other words, because my choice itself is within His sovereignty, "God's guidance" is the expression of faith that He will surely lead me in the best direction.[40]

Now, I hope you will be free from the anxiety of "what if I choose the wrong mate?" We are not the kind of beings who fatefully meet a perfect mate. (You have to get rid of the silly scenes from movies and TV shows!) No matter who you choose to marry, you shouldn't think that everything depends on your choice itself. Ponder the cause of your anxiety. Isn't it because you give all meaning to your "act" of choosing him/her? And isn't it because you think that the happiness of your married life depends on the present state of the person you choose?

We need to turn our attention to the "married life" rather than our choice about marriage. The act of choice is important, but the mar-

★

40) In the Bible, God's guidance experienced by the apostles and the prophets is different from ours. In their cases, it should be understood as special guidance related to the history of redemption in the context of the completion of writing the Bible. In other words, because of the great nature of the revelation that God directly revealed to them, it should be viewed as God's "will" without any personal choice.

ried life after that creates much more significant meaning and happiness in marriage. In this process, we often experience God's good leading. Moreover, we must remember that the "will" of God applies to married life. The holy will of God, over which we have no choice, is evident in marriage.

That is to say, it is God's will for marriage to testify to the mystical union of Christ and the church with the whole body of a couple. The husband must love his wife as Christ loves the church, and the wife should obey her husband as the church does for Christ (Eph. 5:22-33).[41] This is the will of God. Of course, the obedience at this time is "submitting to one another out of reverence for Christ" (5:21).

In any case, we should not say that the matter of personal choice is God's will. Otherwise, you will be guilty of shifting the responsibility of marriage to God. God's will is always holy, always good, and always without fail. In spite of our free choices, God will perfectly accomplish His will no matter what the consequences happen to be. He controls all situations and accomplishes His will "mysteriously," despite our free will not being violated.

In summary, we have to give up the thought that I need to find a specific mate God appointed for me in advance. Also, we must not mistake choosing him/her with our free will as if it were a dimension

---

41) Just because there is no expression of God's "will" in the text, we should not assume that it is not God's will for marriage. As already mentioned, the verses that take on the universality of the life of faith are the revealed will of God to us.

of God's will. Rather, it is clearly God's will that we freely choose a mate with our free will.[42] And we must focus more on married life than on the act of choice about marriage. Why? Because we can finally practice God's will about marriage. I hope you will soon be freed from fatalistic thinking and a wrong understanding of God's will.

42) 이재욱, 「나의 선택과 하나님의 뜻」 (서울: 좋은씨앗, 2019), 114.

1. To what extent are you aware of God's vision in your daily life?

2. Do you have a lifelong mission that you are sure God has given you? If you don't have one yet, please share how you would like to set your mission firstly in relation to the current community.

3. If you are currently dating, how often do you talk about God's vision and each other's mission?

4. Have you ever thought that God appointed a specific mate for you in advance? Now that you know it's not true, how would you like to meet your mate?

5. Explain again in your language how you should understand God's will and your choice.

Chapter 4.

Loving God &
Loving Mate

There was a couple who loved each other passionately and devoted to the life of faith. One day, the brother started to get into trouble. He was happy to love her more and more, but he began to feel sorry to God at some point because he seemed to "meditate" her all day long. Even while he read the Bible, if the same letter as her name came up, his heart pounded for no reason, and even while he prayed, her face continued to pop up.

Even as the brother felt such a happy moment, there was a growing sense of guilt deep down in his heart because he thought he loved her more than God. After some solemn contemplation, one day, he made a serious decision. He gathered the courage to share his resolve and contacted her. Then he carefully spoke out.

Sister, these days, I'm getting really serious. I think I love you more than God. So I guess I'll have to be away for a while or reconsider our relationship.

She was perplexed to hear his word. As a couple who usually regards faith as the highest value, she had to accept his decision, although it was difficult. It seems that they are a truly proud and tearful couple.

This story is an episode that young Christians may experience once or twice when dating passionately. In particular, the more confident you are of good faith when dating for the first time, the more you encounter it. In fact, it is also a failed love story of mine.

Let's consider the brother's reaction for a moment. Does his decision seem like an example of a noble faith? Is there any problem with his understanding of God while he loved her? There is a big problem in my opinion.

First, he recognizes that loving her and loving God are conflicting concepts. In other words, he premises that loving her will make him love God less. However, these two concepts are not in conflict with each other. Rather the opposite. The more he loves her truthfully, the greater his love for God will be. I call this principle the "convergence of love." That is to say, the more he loves her, the more his love eventually converges to God.

As I said, I loved my girlfriend that way when I first started dating. I thought she must not be my idol, so I began to push her away deliberately from my heart where God is. At that time, I thought she seemed to be in place of God in my heart. Anyway, I was secretly proud of myself for making a difficult decision because I was satisfied with my heart to love God more than her.

But the truth is that the defense mechanism was at work in my heart. Because I had never loved God as fervently as I had ever loved her, I was embarrassed by my burning heart for her, which was not with God. In other words, I was panicking that my growing fervent heart for her might devour God, so I activated a defense mechanism in my heart.

Looking back now, I was so naive and ignorant of dating at that time. If we had to date that way, no one would ever succeed in dating or marrying. Suppose such an inner state towards the opposite sex is idolatry. In that case, we must not date or marry all our lives because we cannot "love" anyone more than God. If so, we have to live content "with God alone," even if the expression is a bit strange.

One day, I looked back on myself. I realized that I had never loved God passionately before. I discovered that I didn't love God in the way of my burning love for her. That is why, when my burning heart arose toward her other than God, I made the mistake of pushing her away instead of reflecting on my life of faith. This fact itself tells that I separated her from God and recognized each other apart.

But the Bible teaches that loving God and loving neighbor are inseparable. What did Jesus say to the lawyer who asked, "Teacher, which is the great commandment in the Law?" (Matt. 22:36).

[37]And he said to him, "You shall love the Lord your God with all your heart and with all your soul and with all your mind. [38]This is the great and first commandment. [39]And a second is like it: You shall love your neighbor as yourself. [40]On these two commandments depend all the Law and the Prophets" (Matt. 22:37-40).

Jesus read the lawyer's intention to test Him and summarized all the laws in two points: "loving God = loving neighbor." The first is to love God and the second is to love neighbor. That is, loving God and loving neighbor can never be separated, and we cannot love only one or the other.[43] That includes all kinds of love for our neighbors. Therefore, even couples cannot be free from this principle.

Then we should think that loving him/her is ultimately loving God. It is because all love converges to God. But because of our fallen nature, it takes some training to recognize that. When we fall into a state of intense sexual arousal towards the opposite sex, we almost unconsciously consider loving God and loving him/her as conflicting concepts. As mentioned earlier, the reason is that we have never experienced intense spiritual arousal (awakening) toward God, which triggers a defense mechanism.

Through my failed love story, I learned how to love God. I realized that I should not only understand God logically and rationally but also love the Triune God passionately as if I loved my mate. It became clear to me that there must be fervent spiritual arousal toward God just as there is intense sexual arousal toward the opposite sex.

I ask Christian couples. While happily enjoying your passionate heart for each other, you should converge your love toward God together. Please do not let the state of sexual arousal towards each other

43) 권율, 『올인원 십계명』 (서울: 세움북스, 2019), 120.

lead to the sin of crossing the line, and use it as a way of loving the Triune God fervently. Please remember that the burning love of couples not only makes the two intimate but also their relationship with the God who always watches over them. Blessings will come upon couples who properly realize "loving God = loving mate."

The Convergence of Sin and The Triangle of Love

I came to realize the "convergence of love" unexpectedly while meditating on Psalm 51. The direction is the opposite, but the principle is the same. As indicated in the heading, this psalm was written when the prophet Nathan came and rebuked David after he had committed adultery with Uriah's wife, Bathsheba. David committed the horrific sin of putting his loyal retainer Uriah to death to cover up that he had committed adultery with Bathsheba. So God sent a prophet to expose his sin. At that moment, David thoroughly confessed his sin before God, the King of Israel, and repented.

In his confession, the expression "Against You, You only, have I sinned" (Ps. 51:4, NKJV) struck my heart one day. David clearly says that he has sinned "only" against God even though he had sinned against Uriah and his wife, Bathsheba. A literal translation of the Hebrew text is the same.

At first, I felt David's confession very strange. Taking this sentence alone, it seems that David sinned only against God and not against them. No one repents in this sense without going crazy.

As scholars explain, it is "a Hebrew expression, meaning that every sin breaks the relationship with God."[44] In other words, the sins we commit eventually all converge toward God and oppose Him. That is to say, the more I sin against others, the more I sin against the God who watches over me. I refer to this as the "convergence of sin."

Then Christian couples must not think that their love is only for each other. As previously argued, all of our daily life is based on the love of God. Even couples' love is meaningless if they leave His love for a moment. Every kind of love in this world has real meaning for us when it touches His love.

Lovers must always be on the lookout to see if their passionate love for each other is turning into sin. Burning love between couples is an excellent way to realize God's love vividly, but it can be reduced to an instrument of sin that blasphemes God's love. It occurs when the love between the two is not converging in "one direction" but is only being expressed towards each other. This will eventually increase the distance between the two because we are beings "standing toward God." Let's break it down with diagrams to help you understand.

★
44) 김정우, 『시편 주석 II』(서울: 총신대학교출판부, 2005), 172.

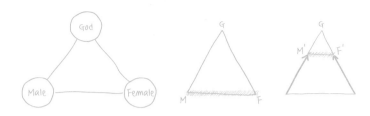

The Triangle of Love[45]

In Chapter 2, I introduced Sternberg's *Triangular Theory of Love*. He took the three components of love as "intimacy, passion, and commitment." But I created *The Triangle of Love* by putting beings (God, male, and female), not concepts. In this case, male and female refer to intimate relationships (unmarried or married) in an exclusiveness with others.

As you can see in the diagram on the left, Christian couples (especially married) form a love relationship with God as the apex. This is not a matter to be agreed or disagreed. From the time God first created Adam and Eve, our very existence was established that way. Why? Because God "has joined together" the two.

If you look at the diagram on the right, you can see that, surprisingly, the closer the couple get to God of the apex, the closer they are to each other. The line segment M'F' is much shorter than the seg-

45) A similar diagram is introduced in some books. But I created the method of explaining it by the change in line segment length through profound meditation 17 years ago.

ment MF in mathematical terms. Conversely, the farther away from God, the longer the distance from each other. It is not just a mathematical concept but a principle of existence that intuitively expresses the relationship of love.

Christian couples must always be aware of the convergence of love and sin through *The Triangle of Love*. First, we must always check whether our burning love for each other is converging toward God. Simply put, we need to examine each other whether we are striving to love the Triune God in the same way that we love each other passionately. To put it as the diagram, the degree of closeness and intimacy between me and him/her is evidenced by each standing closer to God.

At the same time, we need to check whether the love between the two is directed only toward each other, excluding God. Suppose their sexual arousal towards each other becomes so intense that they are unaware of the existence of God. In that case, they are definitely on the verge of convergence of sin. As seen in *The Triangle of Love*, in this case, you and he/she feel intensely in love with each other. Still, in reality, they are each farther from God, and in the end, the distance between them is also far apart. We'll study how dangerous it is in Chapter 5.

It's Not a Division-Allotment Concept!

We are accustomed to dividing and allotting, perhaps because of our fallen nature. We always objectify the existence of others centering on ourselves, giving each of them a different value. We do not think that everyone is in a relationship centering on God as the first cause. Simply put, we lack the ability to see ourselves and others as one in God, centering on Him.

That's why that kind of reaction appears when we love God and people. When I first started dating, I thought of it as the concept of giving as much to God as possible out of all the love I have. For example, if my whole love is 100, I thought I must give 80-90 to God and give the other 10-20 to her. If my passion of faith cooled and I gave 40-50 to God, I started to feel apologetic from then on. It's because I think I love her more than God.

As previously argued, this kind of concept is an error that separates "loving God" from "loving mate." Moreover, the concept of "the total love that I have" is another fallacy to put the source of love in me. In this case, I cannot look at him/her and myself centering on God in Him, and I am in a state of allotting different values to each of the objects I set centering on me.

But the source of the love I have is from God. According to St. Augustine, that God is the Holy Spirit called "Love."[46] In other words, with the love that was poured out on me through the Spirit, I now respond lovingly to God. However, when I feel that my faith is getting stronger, I would misunderstand it as the concept of having to "make" my love and give it to God. At this point, the compulsion is instilled, namely, to allot differently "all the love I have" to each one.

This concept of dividing and allotting love is not God-centered but I-centered. Because love is God, the "love that I have" in Him cannot be divided unless God is divided. Moreover, suppose I clearly recognize that the love I have comes from God. In that case, I will focus on how God, who is love, watches me and him/her, rather than dividing and allotting it centering on me. Only when we change our thinking like that, we can properly practice "loving God = loving mate."

Therefore, you should not look for the fundamental power to love your mate in the passion or sexual arousal that you create. Those are excellent ways to make you fall in love with him/her. Still, remember that those will change as times go by. A couple in burning love may be offended by such words. But for the married like me, it just makes sense.

The power to love mate must be found in the Holy Spirit, who is love and dwells within us. In this way, the more I love him/her, the more I realize that the Holy Spirit in me loves him/her, and on

---

46) St. Augustine of Hippo, "On the Trinity," in *St. Augustine: On the Holy Trinity, Doctrinal Treatises, Moral Treatises,* ed. Philip Schaff, trans. Arthur West Haddan, vol. 3, *A Select Library of the Nicene and Post-Nicene Fathers of the Christian Church, First Series* (Buffalo, NY: Christian Literature Company, 1887), 216.

the contrary, I know that the same Holy Spirit in him/her loves me. Ultimately, this principle is to converge a couple's love toward God. Through that love, they will eventually look at God together.

When we love him/her, we must no longer fall into the "division-allotment concept" that separates God from us. All the responses of love, including sexual arousal, must be God-centered. With a little training, all Christian couples can and should do so. I desire that revival of a God-centered view of dating will take place.

Do Love God Much More!

All Christian couples must love God much more. As mentioned previously, it is because the heart that loves each other flows out of the heart that loves God. In a general sense, it can be said that the power to love him/her arises in my heart. But my heart at this time is based on a sexual attraction to him/her or a state of intense sexual arousal.

Of course, I do not regard such reactions towards the opposite sex as taboo or impure. Those are natural bodily reactions when we love. And it's an excellent way to make a couple love each other. I'm concerned that if we do not put such reactions in their place with God's love, they may lead to "convergence of sin." As previously argued, loving God and loving mate are inseparable. Because of this characteristic, couples' deviance that is not based on God's love immediately leads to sin against Him.

So Christian couples must be able to love God much more vividly! When you love God passionately, you can look at him/her properly based on that love. In particular, sexual reactions and attraction towards each other must be appropriately expressed and controlled in light of that love. Never be deceived by the modern culture of freely expressing what you want to do. This seems to liberate and love oneself but is actually an act of pushing God's sovereignty during the dating.

There is one thing that should not be misunderstood here. You should not think that the more you love God, the more your sexual attraction to your lover will disappear. By no means have I ever said of loving God more to extinguish a sexual reaction towards him/her! This thought is a dichotomy that separates loving God and loving him/her.

Couples must love God passionately because they should put those reactions towards each other to their original place before marriage. Our innate power never controls intense sexual arousal. People who have experienced "burning love" in dating know what it means intuitively. Even after marriage, if you are not faithful to the covenant between husband and wife, you may fall into such a state toward another person. In this case, regardless of the reason, you are committing a crime against your spouse and God.

Therefore, Christian couples must try to love God more than

anyone else. Those who are angry about it or reject it are in a state of reluctance to acknowledge God's sovereignty in dating. You need to realize that you can only love him/her "right" when you love God passionately. Based on God's love, we must put our sin-contaminated desires on the original track. You should try hard to avoid the thought that if you become conscious of God during dating, he/she will be reluctant.

Now you might be asking how to love God passionately. So I'm going to introduce my episode. It's a shameful confession. After breaking up with my "first love," I came to love God vividly. For the first time in my life, I was blinded by a woman and lost my mind for a while. The most striking reaction at that time was that I remember her words all day and all night long.

Funny enough, I did not stop with simply recalling and "meditating" on her words. When I met her and chatted with her, and she said she liked something, I immediately remembered it and later bought it as a gift for her. Her words had tremendous power to spur my actions. If you don't know what I mean, you must not have been in burning dating yet.

Unfortunately, the relationship ended due to my inexperience. Then I began to think of God seriously. Of course, we talked about God's love often during dating. Still, I misunderstood it as the "division-allotment concept" previously mentioned. (That's why this book includes many stories of my dating failures.) After the breakup, I began to examine my faith seriously, and I looked back on whether I really loved God.

In a general sense, I loved God just as little children love their parents. Until the children are mature, they cannot love their parents with the love that comes from the depths of their hearts, and they cannot express deep love that is vivid and real.

After breaking up with her, I wanted to love God to that level. I wanted to experience the thrill of being with her, even in my fellowship with God. More than anything else, I wanted to express the heart of listening to and obeying her words, to God as well.

So I started praying. While praying, I could focus on the Word of God. I realized anew that His "love letter" is the Bible for me and all of us. What I already knew was taking me to a completely different level than before.

There is one sentence that I realized then and organized myself. There is nothing new about it, but it came to me as a completely new sentence at that time.

If you say "I love God" but don't read the Bible, it's like saying to the loved one, "I love you, but I don't care what you are saying!"

Outward evidence of loving God is shown in our closeness to His Word. Why? Because the existence of God and His Word can never be separated. Since then, I have read the Bible, meditated on it, and recited it with great determination. I prayed that if I did not read the Bible even for a day, I would rather not sleep. I learned that the most basic way to love God is to love His Word and respond faithfully to His Word. Also, I realized that I must listen to His Word and discipline myself to pray to live up to the Word. I came to know this simple principle only after breaking up with my first love.

Anyway, I started to love God so passionately and vividly since then. There were many cases where I was caught up in the Word of God and stayed up all night without knowing it. Perhaps because the Holy Spirit stimulated my soul through the Word, I experienced a state of intense spiritual arousal (awakening) in His presence. This is just as a couple in burning love is intensely attracted towards each other.

I hope that Christian couples can experience such a state frequently. When the two together experience a state of intense "spiritual" arousal, that's where the control to properly desire each other comes from. In addition, while naturally enjoying sexual attraction towards each other, strong reason is created that converges each other's love toward God. Moreover, out comes a holy conviction that God will lead their dating beautifully regardless of the outcome.

1. If you are dating, have you ever felt guilty because you seem to love him/her more than God?

2. Have you ever loved the Triune God vividly and passionately as if you loved him/her? If not yet, are you interested in doing so in the future?

3. Describe what it is to feel intensely in love with each other but to be actually distant from each other.

4. How should we recognize the relationship between God, me, and him/her so as not to fall into the division-allotment concept?

5. What is your outward evidence of loving God? Diagnose yourself honestly by comparing the way you love him/her.

Chapter 5.

Physical Contact and Symptoms of Love

Nowadays, if we insist on purity before marriage, we are often treated as fools. If you look at some statistics, there is not much difference in the consciousness of premarital purity between young Christians and non-Christians. In certain groups, it is even worse in the church. Increasingly, even within the church, the consciousness of premarital purity is crumbling. Because young people don't take bed seriously before marriage, a young adult pastor of a megachurch in Seoul gave guidance like this: You are allowed to sleep together if you are getting married anyway. It was a story more than ten years ago. That is what I heard directly from a brother who attended the church.

However, I don't want to compromise on the fundamental desire of young people. Why? Because that is the core of Christian dating that makes a difference between us and the world. I don't want to argue about premarital purity from a developmental psychology perspective. Even from that point of view, I can prove the validity of premarital purity. Still, if the meaning of marriage and purity is not based on the Bible, there is a risk that it will end up in a consuming debate.

The Bible's meaning of purity is not only related to physical relationships but also to the vulgar thoughts, words, and deeds that come from the heart. Just because you didn't sleep with your lover before marriage doesn't mean you have kept the purity completely.

But neither should we undermine that keeping physical purity is the greatest of those. Adultery of the heart is a great sin, but adultery of the body is a much more serious sin. Remember this word: "The body is not meant for sexual immorality, but for the Lord, and the Lord for the body" (1 Cor. 6:13b). It means our bodies must be kept pure for the Lord's sake! We must not think that all sins are the same. That is, whether you commit it with your heart or your deeds, you must not regard that as the same sin anyway. Furthermore, you should not use this as an excuse to become insensitive to premarital purity. We must always be conscious that not all sins are equally abominable. [47]

Confessing the Triune God as "my Lord" is best expressed in my fundamental desire problem. Unless I surrender the very thing I hate to yield to God's sovereignty and His holy will, I am not yet fully submissive to His rule. This applies not only to young people but also to married men and women like me.

I once read Elisabeth Elliot's *Passion and Purity* and was shocked. Her husband is missionary Jim Elliot, who was martyred at the Huaorani tribe of Ecuador at the young age of 28 in 1956. The book vividly depicts the dating story between the two until they got married.

There seem to be many things that young people these days do not

47) WSC, Q. 83. Are all transgressions of the law equally heinous? A. Some sins in themselves, and by reason of several aggravations, are more heinous in the sight of God than others.

agree with emotionally. This is because her dating style is genuinely like a "fool." However, if you look at the book's contents, it seems that the U.S. where Elliot lived was not much different from the current atmosphere in Korea. Students asked the blatant question, "How can we marry someone we've never kissed." She even refers to the atmosphere at that time as "a generation . . . that nearly everybody goes to bed with everybody."[48]

We can't necessarily say that Elliot's dating method is 100% correct. Still, the way she loved him before marriage sets a truly outstanding example for today's Christian young adults. When it comes to loving him, she always recognizes God simultaneously, and the way she cares for the loved one to focus more on God is truly impressive.

> I did not want to turn Jim aside from the call of God, to distract his energies, or in any way to stand between him and a thoroughgoing surrender. This was what I understood real *love* to mean. "And love *means* following the commands of God. This is the command which was given you from the beginning, to be your *rule of life*."[49]

Her attitude is a God-centered dating that is too drastic for us today. Rather, I think that such a view of dating is necessary for Chris-

★

48) Elisabeth Elliot, *Passion and Purity: Learning to Bring Your Love Life under Christ's Control* (Grand Rapids, MI: Revell, 2021), 127.
49) Ibid., 129.

tian young adults. These days, self-centered dating is becoming the "norm" to the point where you can't even recognize it yourself. When they feel that their sexual desires are restrained, they start to feel disgusted. In their dating, there is no room for the kingdom of God and His vision to intervene.

What do you think of Elliot's saying, "I did not want to turn Jim aside from the call of God, to distract his energies . . ."? Doesn't our nature teach that the burning sex of unmarried men and women is one of the greatest obstacles to our relationship with God? Does Elliot, who thoroughly controlled her lust for kissing before marriage, look like a person with different nature from us?

I hope you do not find within ourselves any cause to keep purity before marriage. Marriage is a means of witnessing the mystical union of Christ and the church, and dating is a process of preparation and training as a partial shadow. Sexual intercourse is permitted only between couples in an irrevocable covenant relationship. Why? Because it is an act of man and woman's sharing everything of each other most intimately and secretly. Sexual pleasure is a gift from God that enables a married couple to recognize each other as one body with their five senses.

As anyone in love knows empirically, being sexually aroused means preparing to disarm every part of me for him/her. It means that my fundamental desires are expressed without wearing any mask. It is an existential moment when my reason and judgment become entirely powerless. This state of the "nakedness of whole being" must be for only one person in the world. Of course, it is on the premise that the one cannot be changed! However, dating is an incomplete union in which he/she is likely to change. Therefore, the unmarried must not disarm each other to share their fundamental desires.

The "nakedness of whole being" on the spiritual dimension is also an expression that characterizes our relationship with God. Why? Because He knows even our deepest secrets and wants to conform all our desires to His glory. Our faith is willing to admit that we are naked before God. It is our faith to humbly admit our "existential sinfulness" without putting on any mask and to seek His mercy. The nakedness of my whole being is the state in which my reason and judgment are completely paralyzed before His grace. So now it is a state in which only Christ on the cross is my everything.

This nakedness of the whole being can never be shared with any idol other than God. Why? Because it is an act of pushing away Christ, who has become my everything. Married life is the scene that best shows it. The covenant of marriage is the most vivid evidence of our covenant relationship with God. In other words, the nakedness of the whole being shared between husband and wife is a mirror that reflects our relationship with God.

Then the "nakedness of whole being" contains the relationships of two dimensions at the same time: Our spiritual purity to one God and our physical purity to one spouse. The concept of purity is complete fidelity towards the "one in a covenant relationship." Therefore, the nakedness of whole being towards him/her before marriage is never allowed. Dating is preparation for covenant marriage and only serves as a partial shadow. In this way, we must find the cause to keep purity before marriage in our relationship with God.

Now, Christian couples must do with all their might to keep the purity before marriage. As the sexual attraction towards each other is intense, I pray that each other's will for purity will also be strong. Please remember that keeping purity before marriage is the best act of recognizing God's sovereignty in dating! I hope you can strive together to ensure that the sexual arousal for each other is functioning properly and is in place until you are married. The more you strive to be pure before marriage, the more it will be expressed as love for your spouse after marriage.

Appropriate Level of Physical Contact (1)

There is an episode from a long time ago. I posed a sensitive question to students while giving a dating lecture at a university's Christian club: "What do you think is an appropriate level of physical contact before marriage?" Then a brother proudly said that if the two love each other, they can have a relationship. Of course, he meant it as sexual intercourse that is only possible between husband and wife.

I was a little perplexed. If the brother was not a Christian, I could have accepted what he had just said. But he was active in a Christian club, so I was somewhat shocked at his answer. The others in the place seemed to agree with him.

The appropriate level of physical contact before marriage is of great interest to Christian couples. I was also like that before getting married. It is natural that a couple in love wants to touch each other. As we saw in Chapter 2, when a man and a woman fall in love, their brains become extremely active, secreting many "love hormones" from their body. Among the hormones, *oxytocin* strongly evokes the craving for physical contact. This is especially true in the early stages of dating.

In the process, couples almost mistake intense sexual arousal for love. Why? Because body reactions happen to him/her, which do not occur to others. So some people think that the standard of loving him/her is to have "deep" physical contact.

Christian couples should definitely know. Physical contact is a useful way to love each other, but don't mistake it for love! Even if they can't agree, I will have to keep on insisting with all my conscience. Love is not a state of sexual arousal caused by the secretion of hormones in our body, and it is just one of the forms to express love.

At this point, I would once again remind you of the concept of love. As mentioned previously, love must be primarily defined as being. Why? Because God is the one who showed the prototype of all love, and God Himself is love (1 John 4:8b). And I argued that this existential love can be expressed in other words as "conceptual love." It discusses the formal aspect of love with the premise of our relationship with God, who is the substance of love.

If we take the two components that make up this conceptual love, namely "will" and "emotion," love is an operation of the will accompanied by emotion. How to understand these two components has been sufficiently covered in Chapter 2, so I will omit it here. The lovers' physical touch almost absolutely involves, especially "emotion" among the two components, so it may be a big obstacle to properly understanding the essence of love. I have repeatedly emphasized that although the emotional component is truly important in love, the emotion itself is not love.

Christian couples should first consider why they want to have physical contact. In general, they think that the deeper they touch, the deeper they get to know each other. But this is not true! The deeper the touch, the stronger the sexual attraction, intensifying the arousal state. At this point, men especially "love" their state of sexual arousal. That is to say, men become more focused on their own sexual arousal than on women's state of heart and reactions.

So, while physical contact becomes a vessel for expressing love, it also may degenerate into a selfish means of indulging our desires. The same goes for married couples. Just because you're married doesn't mean you're free to touch indefinitely. Suppose you do not express your love "for" your spouse but only focus on satisfying your own sexual desires. In that case, it is an insult to love and becomes a terrible sin to "love" your desires.

Therefore, lovers must exercise strong restraint in physical contact that maximizes their emotions. The emotion of love has real meaning when a couple loves simultaneously the God who watches over them both. God values the emotional state of lovers, but when the emotion becomes so hot that they become unaware of God's existence, He unleashes a "fire of jealousy" towards the couple. Of course, this is not the level of jealousy that we humans are jealous of! God is so jealous for our sake because all believers, including couples, must be conscious of God's love to enjoy true happiness.

Appropriate Level of Physical Contact (2)

If so, what is the appropriate level of physical contact before marriage? In conclusion, it is not possible to set its standard uniformly. Why? Because each country, each culture, each person has a difference. Nevertheless, we must set a minimum guideline for physical contact and a final point that cannot be compromised.

First, the guideline should be a standard that enables a couple to be conscious of and love God simultaneously, who watches over them. That is because, as demonstrated in *The Triangle of Love* in the previous chapter, when lovers each distance themselves from God, their relationship eventually also becomes more distant. Don't be fooled into thinking that your relationship has grown closer and deeper just because of sexual attraction. You must keep in mind the principle of existence that if your relationship with God becomes alienated, your relationship with your lover will also become distant.

If you feel the urge to burn with desire for each other during physical contact, forget God's existence, and ignore His word about purity, stop immediately. However, in this state, it is almost impossible to stop touching. If you keep on touching to indulge your sexual arousal regardless of his/her state of heart, stop immediately. This is not an expression of love but is merely selfishness that "loves" your desire.

Because of this intense nature of physical contact, each person reacts differently. Some ministers even forbid it thoroughly because of its irresistible force. Some even repented all night for holding her hand "once" while dating before marriage. In some churches, dating is allowed with the permission of the session, and marriage is conducted under the leadership of the session. It's hard to believe, but it's not an old story, and it's happening recently.

We should respect the decisions of such people and such churches. However, it cannot be applied uniformly to all couples. If they force their "absolute" methods on others, I would call them "legalists." Of course, it is one of the necessary methods for couples who are fundamentally vulnerable to sexual reactions. However, if all physical contact could never be allowed before marriage, it would have been written somewhere in the Bible. But there is no such record.

Those vulnerable to physical touch need to exercise greater restraint than others. It was hard for me to hold her hand during dating before marriage because my heart pounded. Perhaps it is because my mother ran away from home when I was young, and there were no women in the house. Such people need to be more careful about physical touch while dating.

On the other hand, there are people who naturally express physical contact and enjoy a sense of security from it. A brother I know has a lot of older sisters at home, so he gets along very naturally with other sisters in that area. It looked so strange to me, so I asked why. He said that he naturally expressed physical touch to his girlfriend, but that didn't cause sexual excitement to skyrocket. Unmarried sisters often find emotional stability through natural touch with their boyfriends in dating.

Since there are so many different attitudes towards physical contact, it is impossible to uniformly set the standard for its expression. So the two in dating must set the standard before God. Some couples hug naturally, while others are hard to tolerate just being arm in arm. Usually, sisters are more disciplined than brothers, so sisters need to control their brothers. Of course, there are more opposite cases than expected.

This method is not perfect either. Due to the nature of single men and women who are vulnerable to the intensity of touch, they rarely control this issue on their own. So, it is an excellent way to voluntarily ask a senior such as a mentor or a minister in charge for guidance, even if it is a little embarrassing. For example, if seen that they violate the appropriate level of physical contact decided together, they ask, "please rebuke us immediately." The two's physical touch is usually done secretly. Still, a slight effect occurs on the conscience remembering what they said. You might want to protest this method, saying, "What are you talking about in a world like this?" However, I am saying to use the function of physical contact as positively and purely as possible before marriage.

Next, I think that "kiss" is the last point of physical contact that cannot be compromised. That is, you must not kiss under any circumstances before marriage. Perhaps some readers might cover this book or boo me because of my word. Nevertheless, I try not to bend my argument in light of the Bible, risking the pastor's conscience.

Surprisingly, it appears in the Bible verses what the *kiss* means. The word kiss refers to an ancient Near Eastern greeting to show love or friendship, intimacy or respect.[50] When used as a general greeting, it does not refer to a deep kiss, a sexual act. Therefore, light kissing as a greeting was established as a custom even between the same sex.

But sometimes, it means a deep kiss between a man and a woman.

---

50) Allen C. Myers, "kiss," in *The Eerdmans Bible Dictionary* (Grand Rapids, MI: Eerdmans, 1987), 629–630.

"Let him kiss me with the kisses of his mouth! For your love is better than wine" (Song 1:2). Moreover, the word *kiss* is sometimes used for God. In this case, it means absolute obedience to God or the deepest level of reverence. A prime example is in Psalm 2:12.

Kiss the Son, lest he be angry, and you perish in the way, . . . (ESV)

Do homage to the Son, that He not become angry, and you perish in the way, . . . (NASB)

As you can see, the psalmist tells us to kiss the Son. The Son here refers to "My Son" in verse 7 in context: the Messiah (i.e., Christ) descended from David. Then this verse tells us to kiss Christ, the Son of God.

Kiss Christ! This means expressing our absolute obedience to Christ and our deepest reverence. That is why the NASB Bible translates it as "Do homage to the Son." That is, when used in relation to God, the meaning of a kiss is to express the deepest reverence for Him.

This kind of reverence is accompanied by extreme intimacy. It premises a state of union with the object of reverence. When we say we revere God, it means that He and I are inseparable. It is the result of faith in the Triune God, and it is also the evidence that we are saved.

The word *kiss* in this context has a religious and spiritual meaning. That is why the Bible expresses "to kiss Baal" (1 Kings 19:18) or "to kiss calves" (Hos. 13:2) when people would have an exclusive relationship or union with others, not God. In other words, that kind of kiss is idolatry and spiritual adultery.

Now, we need to organize the meaning of "deep kiss," not just a general greeting. Since the meaning of a deep kiss between a man and a woman is not specified in the Bible, I will approach it in a way that corresponds to us from the meaning of a kiss in relation to God. In Chapter 2, the relationship between "faith and works" of salvation and "will and emotion" of love were applied in correspondence. Similarly, we can apply it to us correspondently from the religious and spiritual meaning of a kiss.

If kissing the Son signifies a deep reverence for Him and a union with Him or an exclusive relationship, the corresponding meaning can also be applied to the act of kissing between man and woman. Because kissing the Son is not a general greeting, so the act of kissing between man and woman in love is not just a greeting. So, kissing him/her means deep respect, a secret union, and an exclusive relationship where others cannot intervene.

This is a relationship that only married couples can enjoy. Why? Because it is the act of expressing the most secret and deepest intimacy towards each other without third parties intervening. Because of the meaning of kissing, unmarried couples who have not yet become "one flesh" must refrain from kissing. Just because modern sensuous and stimulating culture takes it for granted, we don't have to follow it.

Christian couples must date as distinct from the world. It is the great mission of Christian dating to express and restrain the most fundamental desires of young men and women with God-centeredness. The act of surrendering the most uncompromising desire to God's sovereignty is the ever so beautiful "tears of obedience." I sincerely desire that all lovers will be able to keep their innocence and purity toward God in all their dating before marriage.

"You Trust Me, Right?"

God created man, male and female. It also means that God created man, but He intended man and woman to be different. That is, the differences of each other are combined to form a person as a whole.

However, men and women are surprisingly reluctant to admit that they are different. When I was in charge of the young adult in the church, I often saw unmarried men and women like that. While serving their community, brothers often think of sisters as brothers, and sisters often think of brothers as sisters. So they often quarreled while planning and running an event.

The differences between men and women are also evident in the dating process. The burning phenomenon towards each other in the early dating stage is the same. Still, there is a big difference in expressing that burning heart. In general, men desire to be faithful to their sexual response and express "in action" to love women. On the other hand, women hide their sexual desire and want men to know their hearts first. Of course, not all men and women react this way. There are guys with strong femininity and girls with strong masculinity.

At any rate, average men want to express it continually towards women when obsessed with their sexual excitement. But the problem is that men think women are the same as men. That is to say, men implicitly believe that women want to express themselves through sexual actions to men just as men are faithful to sexual response. Men are almost convinced that women also love men by physical touch, just as men express it intensely.

On the other hand, if the average single women are attracted to men, women will be more careful of their behavior in front of men, hiding their heart. (Of course, it's a little different for women who have sexual experience or are married). But women implicitly think that just as they are wary of sexual attraction, men want to treat women that way too. Women are almost convinced that men feel loved enough just by being with women rather than by excessive touch.

Unfortunately, the differences between men and women cause many problems in the dating process. Of course, if this difference is put in place by loving God, there is no problem. It is not the purpose of Christian dating to eradicate the different sexual responses of unmarried men and women. By what authority can we take away the unique reaction mechanism of the body that God created. By no means!

However, you must always examine yourself so that the different reaction mechanisms may not lead to sin. In particular, I beg on my conscience to the unmarried sisters. Don't ever be fooled by men's words, "You trust me, right?" It means that they are trying to coax you in order to express their sexual desires to the end. Their belief is working now, namely, that you will eventually like excessive touch and even sexual intercourse.

At this moment, many sisters are thinking this way: "Because he loves me, he will cherish and consider me even in sexual expressions." It's a complete illusion! If I were your older brother, I would have scolded you so hard to come to your senses right away. As soon as the words, "You trust me, right?" come out of a man's mouth, just say goodbye. If he is angry or clings to you more, please do not look back and clean it up with a single stroke. Why? Because his purpose and direction of dating are entirely focused on his own sexual desires.

Of course, some men use trickery to reassure her and make her trust themselves. At first, they only express the level of physical touch that she accepts. Still, from a certain point on, the level gradually increases. It's the way they slowly tame her to get stability. This is a classic grooming technique.[51] If you don't pay attention, at some point, you will get used to it without realizing it, and you will conform to their intentions. For this reason, unmarried sisters must share their physical contact with their married seniors or parents. You should often seek advice from such people to protect yourself.

It seems like I attack men only, so I should mention the opposite this time. Surprisingly, I saw some girls couldn't control their desire when doing dating counseling. It was a story a long time ago. A brother was very stressed out by her constant demands, and he had to run to her bedroom right away when she called. At first, I thought he was joking. But when I heard the whole story, it was actually repeatedly happening. Although the two were active in a Christian club together, they were already in a state of indulging in physical touch beyond its limit.

Likewise, if Christian couples are not alert, they are no different from those in the world. The whole process and direction of dating will be centered on their sexual desires. If they feel like their desires are being restrained, they will be outrageous and have antipathy. The reason they get angry is simple. That's because they don't think that they can concede their dating. They don't care about God's sovereignty and vision.

Indeed, those couples must come to their senses before it's too late! They should immediately start training to surrender their fundamental

51) "Grooming is a series of manipulative behaviors that the abuser uses to gain access to a potential victim, coerce them to agree to the abuse, and reduce the risk of being caught." For more details, see this website: https://www.health.com/relationships/what-is-grooming-sexual (accessed January 8, 2022).

desires to God's sovereignty. They need to awaken the spiritual sense of longing for God-centered dating. I sincerely hope they can restore the confession of "We do only believe in God!" instead of "You trust me, right?"

True Symptoms of Love

Even a Christian couple cannot be free from normal sexual reactions between men and women. God did not make His children like angels. Unmarried men and women are bound to be sexually drawn and attracted to each other, whether they believe in Christ or not. Unless congenitally disabled in sexuality, unmarried young people naturally experience sexual arousal during dating.

So we must not fall into extreme asceticism. I once felt guilty and tormented by my sexual reactions toward my girlfriend during dating. I treated myself almost like a beast, thinking, "How could I react that way towards the loved one?" Thinking about it now, I am very ashamed of how ignorant I was in dating.

It should not be misunderstood that the biblical standard of dating is to extinguish the sexual reaction and attraction to the lover. Traditionally, many churches have been implicitly accustomed to such thinking. The older generation is closer to the "ascetic view of dating." (Of course, I will also tell you that there are exceptions.) As a reaction to this, the current generation is almost closer to the "hedonistic view of dating." They jump on the world's culture and think it's rather strange to suppress their desires.

Christian couples should not lean towards extremes. While enjoying a natural sexual attraction and reaction towards each other, you must work hard to keep it in place until marriage. Never be fooled by the world's norm that if you love, you can give him/her everything! Why? Because evidence of love doesn't depend on such things.

We need to listen to what the Bible says about the nature of love. I'll mention it again because we often distort and forget. No matter what the Bible says, our sinful nature is willing to succumb to the body's reaction. Although we seem to be very logical and rational based on the Bible on the outside, in the inside we are weak sinners who fall uncontrollably in the face of fundamental desires.

What does 1 Corinthians 13 say about love? "Love is patient and kind; . . . it is not arrogant or rude. It does not insist on its own way; . . . Love bears all things, believes all things, hopes all things, endures all things."

Those are attributes that encompass all kinds of love. Therefore, the love of couples should also be based on these words. We should not believe that evidence of love lies in sexual reactions or attraction toward each other. As I keep emphasizing, the state of sexual arousal fades over time. It would be like preaching to deaf ears for a couple burning in love. But I want to keep reminding you. Please don't mistake sexual arousal as if it were a true symptom of love! Such a state is always variable due to the limitations of our bodies. He/she may not always be attractive to your eyes.

We must pursue the unchanging attribute of love. Christian lovers should be patient, kind, not rude, and not insist on their own way. Also, they should bear all things, believe all things, hope all things, and endure all things. The best way to practice these attributes of love is to strive for premarital purity. It is to thoroughly submit to the sovereignty of God the most difficult fundamental desire for burning single men and women to yield.

In a sense, couples in dating are more likely to practice those attributes of love than are married couples. The married are easily angered, rude, and often have a hard time bearing each other. It's maybe because of the belief that the fence of the covenant protects them when they get married. If you don't know what I'm talking about, ask married seniors or your parents. However, we must endure when dating so that our burning hearts may not lead to sin. We must tolerate each other and not seek our own interests in order to dream the future together. You have to believe in "love" even when sexual arousal is gone, and you have to hope all things and endure all things even in an uncertain relationship.

Are young Christians who are dating really seeking such love? Or do you think of him/her as a likely person when he/she is attractive to your eyes? Or do you express disappointment when he/she does not meet your standard? Still, are you confessing that you love God unchangingly no matter what the circumstances? It's a blatant lie! The way you love God is the same way you love him/her. I have demonstrated in detail in Chapter 4 that loving God and loving mate can never be different.

Are you currently "loving" him/her conditionally? Then you need to realize that you are "loving" God exactly that way. Have you ever prayed as if bargaining with God in the name of a vow? Wouldn't you respond to God only when He gives grace according to your standard? If you are "loving" God in this way, you are "loving" him/her exactly that way.

All married people, including me, are the same. Rather, the way married people love God manifests more openly than when dating before marriage. The safe fence of the covenant shows the degree of love for your spouse as it is. We forget the mission of the couple to testify to the mystical union of Christ and the church, and we begin to look at our spouses based on our feelings and thoughts. This is our "present" state of love for God. Nevertheless, we confess that we love God unconditionally and unchangingly. What an abomination!

To be honest, even as I write this book, I am very afraid. That's because my readers may think of me as someone with a different nature. As a pastor, I am no different. I realize and understand such a principle, but I cannot dare say that I practice it 100% in my actual married life. As Christ loves the church, I have to love my wife unconditionally. Still, I have been frequently disappointed because I do not love so in my daily life.

Nevertheless, thanks to the mercy of the Lord, I appeal to all Christian lovers. I hope you find the true symptoms of love based on the "Love Chapter." If you want to properly love one person for the rest of your life after getting married, you must constantly train yourself with the true nature of love from the time you start dating. During married life, you will often think or say, "I love you, nevertheless." What does that mean? That is, "Even though you are far short of my standards and your appearance is entirely different from what I thought, I still endure everything and love you."

Please do not look for evidence of love or symptoms of love in the variable matters. Sexual attraction or arousal can only temporarily help you love. But it cannot in itself be a true symptom of love. Again, if you love him/her properly, you must be patient according to the apostle's teaching. In loving God passionately, you must not be rude to him/her. And while dreaming of the future together for the sake of God's kingdom and His vision, you must believe everything, hope everything, and endure everything. Heavenly blessings will come upon couples who pursue this kind of love!

This time I am going to cover a more sensitive topic. It is about the meaning and function of sexual desire inherent in all people. I am not an expert in this area. Nevertheless, as a married pastor, I would like to share with my readers the traces of my thoughts in light of the Bible and doctrine as I meditate seriously.

The sexual desire that God has bestowed upon us is a beautiful thing. If you consider sexual desire taboo or unclean, you deny God's act of creation, which gave it to humankind as a gift. The problem lies in our distorted attitudes toward sexual desire and the wrong way we use it.

As often mentioned, sexual desire is a gift from God that enables a loving couple to vividly perceive their unity with each other through their five senses. Although the symptom of love is not equal to sexual desire, it is undoubtedly one of many reactions that occur when you love him/her. It is especially noticeable when they have a stormy love during dating or when a couple loves each other at the early stages of marriage.

At this point, your body's reaction is in the highest state of arousal towards him/her. Thoughts towards him/her keep you awake all day long with full energy and even wake you up sober through the night. When I was dating my first love, I "meditated" on her words all day and night. Of course, now that I'm married to another woman, I've forgotten what I was thinking at that time.

Anyway, when you are filled with the sexual desire that comes from love, you love him/her in a very real and vivid way. In this case, no artificial methods are required at all. So naturally, you have no choice but to love him/her. It feels rather strange to be obligated to treat him/her.

In this way, the sexual desire that God has given is functioning positively in loving a mate. But God didn't just give us sexual desire only to be content with loving him/her. As the Bible testifies, our body is a temple where God dwells and is an "instrument for righteousness" in which we must glorify God (1 Cor. 6:19-20; Rom. 6:13). It says to use every member and every part of our body to reveal the glory of God.

If so, sexual desire should also be a means of witnessing God and worshiping Him. Does that sound too absurd? John Piper, a world-famous evangelical theologian and pastor, says the same thing. He insists on making all our physical desires a means of worship.[52] If he did a good job of demonstrating sexual desire as a means of worship, I would like to address how sexual desire itself serves as a projection between God and us.

This has been partially mentioned earlier. Now I'm trying to put it together and organize it systematically. First of all, just as there is a

52) John Piper, *This Momentary Marriage*, 121.

sexual desire toward a loved one, there is a spiritual desire toward the beloved God. That is, we express our "holy desire" toward the Triune God. If you are possessed by the former, you will be filled with sexual desire, and if you are possessed by the latter, you will be filled with the Holy Spirit.

I said that when filled with the sexual desire that comes from love, lovers experience the highest arousal for each other. If you don't know what I'm talking about, you've never had a burning love yet. Sexual arousal is primarily a means of burning in love for each other. However, we need to go one step further here. Why? Because ultimately, God must be witnessed through every part of our body.

Therefore, the sexual arousal towards each other must ultimately be a mirror that reflects the spiritual arousal (awakening) towards God. Simply put, this way of loving him/her vividly with five senses should eventually become a way to love God practically and passionately.

Do you think this is getting more absurd? The Puritan master Jonathan Edwards (1703-1758) excelled in this method. He felt the sweet love of God and experienced it like a flood of water.[53] He was overwhelmed by the amazing love and vividly lived a daily life of loving God. He even made 70 resolutions, and through them, he exerted effort to express his holy desire toward God.

Can only Edwards love God that way? Not at all. To varying de-

---

53) 백금산 편, 『조나단 에드워즈처럼 살 수는 없을까?(개정판)』 (서울: 부흥과개혁사, 2003), 99-101.

grees, any bride of Christ can and should love Him that way! Though not always, I often experience a state of spiritual arousal. There are times when I am caught up in the overflowing love of God and have trouble sleeping all night long. Reading or studying the Bible or writing down the grace of God experienced in daily life, I spend the night praying in the highest state of awakening. I don't know why. As Romans 5:5 says, it seems that God's love was poured into my heart through the Holy Spirit.

I learned this principle after breaking up with my "first love." (I have already mentioned in Chapter 4.) Just as I reacted immediately and excitedly to her words, I wanted to respond to God that way. Until then, I seemed to love God only in words and understand Him superficially. From then on, I wanted to love God as vividly and passionately as if loving a girlfriend. Thankfully, God heard my prayer, and I often experience the vivid outpouring of His wonderful love through the Holy Spirit.

In this way, the sexual desire inherent in us should be a mirror that reflects the spiritual desire toward God. You can train it together with your spouse on the most intimate and deepest level. You should enjoy the happiness of expressing the deepest level of spiritual desire to God while enjoying the highest level of sexual desire (kiss, sexual intercourse) with him/her. Everything is permitted within the framework of the covenant. Even our fundamental desires must be turned into instruments of righteousness that testify to God!

Next, we must keep in mind that sexual desire degenerates into idolatry the moment it combines with sinful nature. Sexual desire is powerfully addictive, and it has a tremendous power to excite the five senses. This quality of sexual desire is an excellent way to make a couple practically "feel" one flesh. Still, when combined with our sinful nature, it makes us indulge in the thrill itself. Why? Because sin directs the object of worship to something other than God.

For this reason, the highest levels of sexual desire (kiss, sexual intercourse) are forbidden before marriage. There are couples who have never had sex. But there are never couples who have had only once, except under special circumstances. The thrill of sexual desire and sinful nature are combined, making their whole personality immerse in it.

If that happens, you are eventually committing spiritual adultery against God. It is because the sexual desire that God gave us as a gift to testify to Himself remains in the pleasure itself that comes from a physical relationship with him/her. In this context, both the unmarried and the married are no exception. Even if a married couple indulges in each other's flesh and pours all their lusts into it, this is blasphemy against the God who gave sexual desire. Of course, as time goes by after marriage, sexual desire takes its place in the normal case.

Lastly, spiritual desire toward God is also reduced to idolatry when it is combined with sinful nature. When I experienced a state of spiritual arousal through the outpouring of God's love, I really felt like I was in paradise. It was as if I felt the union with the Triune God vividly through my five senses. Nothing in this world came into my consciousness, and I was filled with only God. I just longed for that moment to go on forever.

But it did not last. It is as if the sexual arousal towards the loved one does not continue. I was very confused at first. As the vivid experience of feeling God's love disappeared, I started to think as if I didn't love God anymore and God didn't love me either. This is the same logic as panicking when love hormones are no longer secreted in dating.

At one time, I struggled in many ways to restore and maintain the spiritual thrill. This is because I mistakenly believed that I love God only when I have a thrilling experience of spiritual desire. It was an excellent spiritual experience. But it combined with my sinful nature, and I was in a state of indulging in itself, not God.

That is why God certainly takes away the state of spiritual arousal when the time is right. God knows very well that we cannot fully love Him that way as long as we are still in our sinful flesh. In my opinion, He is granting us a sinless resurrection body on the Last Day so that we may enjoy the highest state of spiritual arousal to the full forever. It is so that we can fully love the Triune God without any influence of sinful nature even when God's love is poured out to the extreme.

Our sexual and spiritual desires must be the means to testify to and enjoy the Triune God fully. Above all, unmarried couples should properly enjoy it within appropriate levels before marriage and strive to control it. Married couples should seek to manifest the mystical union of Christ and the church by sharing everything in the covenant! I am convinced that when the fundamental desires of Christian lovers are thoroughly subordinated to God's sovereignty and His will, an actual conversion of Christian dating will occur.

1. Do you agree with the idea that you must keep purity before marriage? If not, why do you think so?

2. What is the appropriate level of physical contact, in your opinion? Please share why you think so.

3. If you are currently dating, are you giving in to the intensity and addictiveness of physical touch? Or do you try to control it properly together?

4. Where do you find the true symptoms of love during dating?

5. Wouldn't you like to express your holy desire for God in the way you are in love with him/her?

Chapter
6.

Church Reality and Actual Dating

As a field minister, I hear more of this saying as time goes on: It's really hard to find a mate in the church. I hear this more often from sisters than from brothers. So, like other young adult pastors, I have a holy burden. I am seriously thinking about how the church's young people can find a good mate, have a beautiful relationship, and get married. The Young Adult Union Retreat and the Pre-Marriage Course, which I frequently attempt to hold, are also part of that concern.

Actually, it is difficult for sisters to find a mate in the church. Not all churches are like that, but there are much more women in the church in general. This is particularly the case for unmarried young people of marriageable age. In a church in Seoul, there is an episode in which ten sisters waged a "prayer battle" over one brother.[54]

There are various reasons why there are so many sisters in the church. In my analysis, it is because the attitudes and patterns of continuing the life of faith are different between men and women. It seems to me that, in general, sisters are more consistent in their life of faith than brothers. Rather than doing it consistently by their will, sisters seem to follow the church's guidance and parents' words comparatively better than the brothers. Of course, there are opposite cases.

Many brothers spend a long time wandering away from their faith, es-

54) 이애경, 「기다리다 죽겠어요」 (서울: 터치북스, 2012), 24-26.

pecially when they go to college and get away from their parents' influence. This is because they begin to be deeply immersed in the stimulating culture outside the church that they have encountered before. They leave their parents and try various deviances at their discretion. In addition to sexual deviance, they expose themselves to cultures that run counter to the values of faith, and in some cases, indulge them for some time. In certain regions and generations, sisters may also show a similar tendency.

Anyway, brothers usually start wandering when they turn 20 years old. There are even cases in which they become mature in faith after the age of 40. For this reason, the proportion of unmarried men and women between the ages of 20 and 40 differs significantly in the church. Since the sisters do not express spiritual rebellion overtly aside from exceptional cases, they remain far more numerous than brothers in the church at that age.

Considering this reality, ministers should wisely guide young people's dating in the church. We need to deeply empathize with how difficult it is for especially sisters to find a believing partner in the church, suggest appropriate alternatives to these practical problems, and teach the faith principles of dating. Otherwise, talking unilaterally with only theological premises will only make conversations with young people more and more difficult.

For a long time, I have included dating-related lectures and meetings in the young adult union retreat and also opened a dating course or pre-marriage course separately from the retreat. In some places, even young people viewed these attempts as secular, but the general response was positive. Even when I was young, I could not have even imagined such a program in the church. It may be because it was a rural area, and the seniors in the church often rebuked us not to turn the chapel into a "dating hall."

Because the negative perception of dating is deeply rooted in the church, our young people have not had the opportunity to acquire a biblical view of dating. So they seem to have not actively tried to date in the church community. As a reaction, many churches started to open dating and marriage courses like sprouting mushrooms from some time ago. In my diagnosis, many cases deal with dating from the perspective of developmental psychology.

Now, from a more balanced perspective, we need to bring the Christian young adults' dating to the surface. Regarding the issue of dating, which is the biggest prayer topic of young adults, church ministers must come together and approach it from multiple perspectives. And as far as the dating issue of young Christians is concerned, it is necessary to break away from the individual-churchism and actually unite across denominations. Local churches should unite to establish young adult union retreats, dating courses, or pre-marriage courses. Rather than lectures led by specific institutions or megachurches, I think it is better to deal with those in a union meeting where young adult pastors cooperate.

In any case, it is becoming increasingly difficult for young people to find a mate in the church. In particular, there are many unmarried sisters in their late 30s or over 40, having difficulty attending the young adult service with younger juniors. It is emerging as an actual concern among young adult pastors. Some even say that a separate department should be created. A church with many young people and a smooth supply of ministers can try such a method, but a church with a small young adult department cannot even dare to do so.

As the title of AeKyoung Lee's book *I'm Dying Waiting*,[55] we need to consider the reality of the young adult in the church seriously. More sisters than expected are "to the point of death" while praying and waiting to meet the future spouse. Some move to other churches because of this problem. Even though the parents are lay leaders in the church, there are cases in which they move to a large church with many brothers because of their parents' suggestion. The brothers who they have been with for a long time in a church do not look like men at all for sisters. Moreover, the ministers constantly "brainwash" them against marrying non-Christians, so our sisters seem to feel constrained in various ways.

To make matters worse, the church binds the sisters with works in some cases. In my view, the most irresponsible minister instills the illusion that a wonderful brother will be given to a sister in return for serving the church. It even makes them think that their future spouse's qualifications are determined by their dedication to God's kingdom and the church. God will severely rebuke such ministers.

Of course, in a few cases, the church's seniors recognize the sisters devoted to their work and introduce them to brothers from other churches, so they date and dramatically get married. But compared to the number of sisters

---

★

55) This is an English translation. The original Korean title is 『기다리다 죽겠어요』.

in the church, such cases are very rare. Now, the church and especially the young adult pastors need to seriously consider and approach the issues of sisters' dating and marriage.

Their dating and marriage issues are ultimately directly related to brothers' dating and marriage. Why? Because dating and marriage require a partner. So, the best way is to counsel the brothers so that they do not leave the church but continue to live the Christian life. It is necessary to educate the brothers thoroughly from their middle and high school years so that they in their 20s and 30s may not wander from the faith. Otherwise, they will become preoccupied with the girls of the world.

However, it is not as easy as we think, perhaps because of the strong secular current of this generation and because of the temperament of brothers faithful to their instincts. The brothers who survive the intense faith training and settle in the church "strangely" try to devote themselves as pastors, missionaries, or staffs of mission organizations. Brothers in this category, to which I belong, are the ones that sisters find most burdensome to meet as marriage partners. That is why it is even more difficult for sisters to find a mate in the church.

Considering this reality and many other reasons, we need to guide young people's dating issues. I teach the principles of this book in a clear tone. Still, I do not blindly judge the reality of young adults based solely on theological premises. There are cases in which they cannot have a date of faith according to this book's principles because they have poor faith. Ministers must first empathize with the hearts of young people and feel their pain. We must not only view them as objects or means of ministry but actively set the stage for dating and an opportunity to be married.

 ## Dating Issue with Non-Christians

As it is difficult to find a mate within the church, young Christians try to find one outside the church. In the field of ministry, sisters always come back to "complain" when I almost forget. They say that they cannot find a mate in the church, no matter how hard they look. Whenever they say that, with the heart of an older brother, I am deeply troubled about how to set the stage for our sisters.

Some sisters end up dating non-Christians, perhaps because they are likely to die while waiting. There are cases in which they date and marry a non-Christian because their faith is infirm, but there are cases in which they cannot help but make such a choice because they cannot wait any longer. Whatever the reason, I am watching with a sad heart. Our sisters worry that such a choice will be reflected as unbelief. But we need to sympathize with them in the circumstance that it is so tough to meet brothers in the church.

Nevertheless, I have principles that cannot be compromised. If they dare say they want to date a non-Christian, I am not blindly opposed. However, I advise them not to marry "while he is an unbeliever." Rather than my advice, the Word of God commands so.

¹⁴Do not be unequally yoked with unbelievers. For what partnership has righteousness with lawlessness? Or what fellowship has light with darkness? ¹⁵What accord has Christ with Belial? Or what portion does a believer share with an unbeliever? ¹⁶What agreement has the temple of God with idols? For we are the temple of the living God; as God said, "I will make my dwelling among them and walk among them, and I will be their God, and they shall be my people.

This text is from 2 Corinthians 6:14-16. Verse 14 clearly says, "Do not be unequally yoked with unbelievers." Of course, this is not only about the marriage issue but the apostle's overall criticism of the uncleanness of the Corinthian church at that time. In particular, it means not to be yoked with those who claim to be saints, oppose the apostle's teachings, and spread the idolatry and immorality of Corinth in the church. Since the issue of fornication was seriously raised in the Corinthian church at that time, it is natural to apply this text to the matter of marriage.

As we see in verse 16, to marry an unbeliever is an abomination that unites our body, the temple of God, with an idol. Because we are united with Christ, our union with unbelievers is like drawing Christ into that place. Verse 15 already says, "What accord has Christ with Belial?"

Since the living God dwells in the homes of married couples and wants them to be His temple (v. 16), how can we break His word and unite with unbelievers? Can you share spiritual fellowship with an unbeliever dreaming of the kingdom of God? Moreover, since God desires to seek Godly offspring through married couples (Mal. 2:15), do you think you can produce Godly covenant offspring through a spouse who does not know God?

Even in a harsh and sad reality, we must set a standard that cannot be compromised. At this point, the church's holiness and the distinction of Christian dating are revealed. Our mission is to subdue even our most fundamental desires to God's sovereignty and to wait patiently for His excellent guidance in the midst of difficult realities.

I am against marrying a non-Christian but not at all against marrying him/her after he/she has been born again into a covenant people. In a way, that's really commendable. But the process of discernment is essential. Before getting married, the community must verify that the brother has genuinely been born again. So, I ask unmarried sisters. If you want to date a non-Christian, you can marry him, but wait for a while until he is baptized and makes a public confession of faith. Some of the couples I've coached have actually done this. The opposite is also true. These days, a brother of good faith often brings a sister from outside the church.

Particularly, because of their nature, men endure almost anything to marry a woman. Even though they are not converted, they are faithful to the church life as if they were members more than the current members. Then, soon after marriage, there are cases in which they show their true colors. Someone I know got married that way but divorced before her baby even began to recognize the daddy's face. The only reason was that he started to become bored with a woman who goes to church and can't live with her anymore.

Of course, most of them do not divorce and continue to live with their non-Christian mate. In the early days of marriage, they love only because the secretion of love hormones is strong. Still, when the influence of the hormones disappears, they start looking for reasons for married life other than love. In particular, the Christian spouse is instinctively inclined to feel spiritual longing. They realize that spiritual fellowship with their closest mate is impossible. From then on, they become frustrated or even regret getting married.

But by then, it is too late. They must cry out to God for the salvation of one soul for the rest of their lives. Also, they should live thinking of their home as "a missionary field." Home should be a mission base for the kingdom of God, not a mission field! They have to live with the cost of sharing the yoke with an unbeliever. Of course, there are some blessed cases where the unbelieving spouse is quickly converted and lives a life of faith together because of the Lord's mercy. However, they spend a really long time trying to evangelize their unbelieving mate in so many cases. A certain female minister I know prayed for all her life over the conversion of her husband, and her prayer was answered not long before she died.

Even so, we must not limit God's providence with our reason.

There is a brother greatly used by God by marrying a sister who had good faith when he was a non-Christian. This is the story of the deceased Elder Young-Gil Kim, the first president of Handong Global University. He was introduced for marriage to a Korean sister while studying in the United States. They dated for a year only through photos and letters. Moreover, it is said that his older brother went out to date the sister for him.[56] And she put forward the condition that the man who will become her husband must attend church. He agreed to do that, so he got married. As time passed, he was really converted! I don't need to mention how God used him.

Since there is such a providence of God, we should not think that everything must fit into our theological premise. Even if the unfortunate choices of marrying a non-Christian are sometimes made, we must believe that God's grace can be poured out, which leads to good results. However, please do not use this exceptional case as an excuse to rationalize your intention to date an unbeliever.

In any case, we should not simply approach the issue of dating a non-Christian. I hope that, if possible, all Christian single men and women will find a believing mate according to the scriptures thoroughly. If you "are forced" to date an unbeliever for practical reasons, please wait until he/she is converted, baptized, and begins a life of

56) 신상목, "[역경의 열매] 김영길〈5〉: 사진으로만 본 신붓감과 1년 편지교제 끝 결혼", 『국민일보 미션라이프』 2016년 6월 16일, http://news.kmib.co.kr/article/view.asp?arcid=0923566809&code=23111513&cp=nv.

faith. Do not have a careless thought that "I will be an exception like the first president of Handong Global University!" Otherwise, you may be spending the rest of your life only evangelizing one soul.

 ## Let's Lower Our Standards a Bit!

Another reason why it is difficult for single Christians to date comes from themselves. Brothers keep on getting caught up in the sense of defeat and are afraid to try dating. Sisters are raising their standards more and more, making it difficult to find a dating partner. Of course, the opposite is also true, so please don't offend each other.

Once, while consulting a sister, I heard about her ideal man: Faith is basically required for her mate, and he has a decent appearance, tall stature, above-average economic power, and a family of faith. And she added like cutting somebody to the quick, saying, "I want to avoid ministers as much as possible." The moment I heard those words, I was convinced that I would never have even started dating her if I had been single. There was nothing that matched her ideal man except for faith.

What does the phrase "faith is required basically" mean? It means that there must be other things besides faith. I have never heard, especially from the sisters, during dating counseling so far, that they want to meet a brother only for their faith. Brothers are generally similar. Please think about it. There aren't many brothers in the church who are satisfying to the sisters' eyes than expected. Those with a firm and passionate faith usually try to become ministers, but this is burdensome for sisters. Those with good-looking faces have an infirm faith. And those with a family of great faith have poor financial power in her sight.

Considering this and that, sisters cannot find a dating partner. There is already a shortage of brothers of marriageable age in the church. I would like to give straightforward advice to the sisters. But I think it will hurt their heart if I do as a male minister. So I would like to recommend a female writer's book that advises sisters like hitting the nail on the head. This book has already been mentioned. Be sure to read the book *I'm Dying Waiting* by AeKyoung Lee. Unlike me, she writes beautifully with an excellent touch, so you will read losing track of time. In particular, please carefully read Chapter 2, "Let's not make excuses because there must be some reason why we didn't get married."

One day, I was really moved by Nick Vujicic's dating and marriage story. As a handicapped body without limbs, he started dating a beautiful sister and married her. Contrary to his thoughts, "I didn't think I could get married even if I do everything else,"[57] he shared a love that went beyond the limits in our sight. Accepting Nick's dramatic proposal, she began her married life. One day, her parents-in-law worriedly asked her, "What if you had a child with no arms and legs?" She replied, "Even if I have five children like Nick, I would love them as I love Nick.[58]

★

57) 닉 부이치치 외, 『닉 부이치치 부부의 한계를 껴안는 결혼』, 정성묵 옮김 (서울: 두란노, 2017), 13.

A dating like that is absolutely impossible by the standards we have set. If God's love and faith in Christ are not our everything, marriage is even more impossible. Nick and his mate are a couple who are crazy about unconditional love, and it is the case in which only faith in God and His love became their everything.

Look closely! Doesn't Nick's sweetheart resemble someone? The One who humbled Himself infinitely for us who are infinitely lowly compared to Him, the One who gave everything to us who are not deserved to be loved, Jesus Christ! Can't you remember the One who willingly endured death on the cross to unconditionally love a sinner like us full of spiritual disabilities? Don't you think the mystical union of Christ and the church is being witnessed through Nick and his wife?

If possible, I wish that Christian young adults will seek such love. I pray that there will be many couples who dream of God's kingdom with only faith. I want them not to find a mate by fitting him/her into the ideal they have set, but to be captivated by God's love poured out through the Holy Spirit. And I hope that they will love and date him/her the way Christ loves us and finally marry the loved one.

Do you think I'm too ignorant of reality? No way! Growing up in an environment of domestic violence and a divorced family, I felt that I would never be able to get married for the rest of my life. I was entirely far from the

---

★
58) 유원정, "'힐링캠프' 닉 부이치치, 아내와 러브 스토리도 '뭉클'", 『CBS노컷뉴스』 2013년 6월 18일, https://www. nocutnews.co.kr/news/1052676.

ideal man of sisters these days. I was carrying a mountain of debt in my family, not to mention being in a family of unbelievers. Moreover, I stuttered severely (fluency disorder), probably because of family strife when I was young. Even now, there is not much difference other than in sermons and lectures.

But at a relatively young age, I experienced God's love deeply. When my father was lying ill, I received evangelism from church members who "accidentally" came to my house and started my life of faith. From then on, I began to believe that even if I had nothing, the Lord was enough for me. Of course, there were times I badly wandered when breaking up with my first love in my early 20s. But captivated by the Lord's love, I was always dreaming of the kingdom of God. Although it would be nice to have a date, I was not confident considering my family environment and economic power. Occasionally, some sisters used to like me with their maternal love. Among them, a sister had been dating me for a while. But she had to break up after a week because of the fierce opposition from her family.

In the meantime, I met my current wife through a church sister's introduction at that time. At the first meeting, I told all the truth. I told her the troublesome family story, my handicap, and everything she would hate to find out later, on the first day of the blind date. It was because she may not like those things anyway and eventually want to break up, or her parents would tell me to break up.

I was about to finish talking without expectations. Out of the blue, she said, "What does all of that matter?" Rather, she comforted me that we could overcome them together if we became lovers. From that day on, our dating began. But she broke up for a while because of her friends' concerns. Surprisingly, our dating resumed again and rapidly developed into marriage. We got married in July 2005, both at the young age of 26.

As Paul confessed, "by the grace of God I am what I am" (1 Cor. 15:10). This is also thanks to my wife's unsparing devotion and hard work. I came to know later that my wife had lowered her standards a lot before she met me, praying for her future mate. If my wife had continued to keep her standards before marriage, I wouldn't be where I am today. After all, sisters need to lower their standards to save a brother like me!

Honestly, the need to lower the standards should be required for both brothers and sisters. Brothers with faith and other qualifications should not consider the sister's physical appearance. As we get older, our appearances become standardized. Also, I hope that sisters should not insist on living alone all their lives if they cannot find a good brother. Even if he looks okay when dating, all the men, including me, are pretty much the same when you get married. There is only the grace of the Lord who has compassion on us.

We all should never forget that Christ lowered His standards infinitely to be our Bridegroom. We must put into practice His words, "just as I have loved you, you also are to love one another" (John 13:34). Please abandon the thought that dating matters are an exception to this word. Like Nick's wife mentioned previously, I sincerely hope that our young Christians will have the "grace" to lower their standards drastically toward each other in Christ.

The Roles of Men and Women in Dating

I dealt with dating, marriage, and the ultimate substance in Chapter 1. In the context of the flow, there is a part that I wanted to deal with later.[59] It is about the roles of men and women in dating. Based on the Bible, we should say that the roles of husband and wife in marriage are distinct. That is, the husband is the head of the wife as Christ is the head of the church, so wives are to submit to their husbands, and husbands must love their wives, just as Christ loved the church and gave Himself for it (Eph. 5:23-25).

Those are not my words, but the words of God spoken through the apostle. So I hope women don't feel offended when the Bible says wives should "submit" to their husbands. It is to do so because of the covenant role that Christ is the head of the church, which must be revealed through the husband in the family. And it never means to submit blindly because of the husband's nature. Suppose the husband does not fulfill the Christlike role and is not faithful to the marriage covenant. In that case, wives have a mission to rebuke their husbands sternly and lead them to Christ.

However, can we say that the roles of men and women are fixed based on this text, even during dating? Not at all. I once coached a couple of college students. They both had good faith, so they made

---

*

59) Chapter 1, page 46.

an excellent example for the Christian club because they were dating soundly. As time passed, their relationship deepened, and it seemed like they were about to get married soon.

But the brother seemed to go too far. This doesn't mean that physical touch was excessive. I mean, his attitude toward dating was as if he were married. He said to the sister, "Our love is a covenant." Also, he had a clear idea of the roles of men and women in dating with his theological knowledge. His idea was based on the Ephesians mentioned earlier. That is to say, he argued that a brother is the head of a sister, and that is what the Bible says about dating.

No way! A man and a woman dating are not yet in a covenant relationship. Unlike marriage, dating relationships can be broken. No matter how much couples love each other, the love they experience during dating is not yet "love" in a strict sense. It is only extreme intimacy due to the strong secretion of hormones. The love the Bible speaks of is covenant love. In other words, it is a "love of virtuous cycle" in which we have to remain faithful to the covenant while loving each other based on the covenant that cannot be broken. It is an exclusive faithfulness that no third party can intervene. This means marriage. We will discuss it in detail in the next chapter.

Therefore, lovers who are not in a covenant relationship cannot claim the fixed roles of men and women based on the Ephesians. Of course, while dating, a brother can love a sister just as Christ loves the church, and a sister can have a brother's protection just as the church is His body. This is not a fixed role based on the covenant relationship but the level of pre-training the contents of the covenant relationship before marriage.

These days, the spiritual capacity of the sisters in the church is increasingly excellent. As mentioned earlier, graduating from high school and being away from their parents can be a deviation for a while, especially for brothers. Many husbands in their 40s have been wandering for 10 or 20 years, but have now finally matured in faith through the constant interest and devotion of their wives. In this church reality, it is almost like a wish for our sisters to expect the deep love and protection of Christ from the brothers while dating.

So our sisters seem to be going through a double hardship in the church. Because of the brothers who have lost their faith or have been "disappeared for a long time," sisters have to undertake a greater ministry in the church. At the same time, they have to make much effort to find a believing mate. Sisters need to nurture infirm brothers spiritually, have a dating relationship, and get married.

This sad reality makes the sisters rather play the role of Christ while dating, and I often see couples who actually have to do that. A brother is continuing his life of faith only because he likes the sister, but she earnestly hopes that his faith will grow a little more. Even though the brother was baptized as an infant and entered a faith, he just looks like a "religious person" in her sight. The sisters who bring in non-Christians are doing everything they can in order to convert the brothers into baptized members.

This is the reality of our churches in many cases. So I want to express my sincere comfort and gratitude to the sisters. The brothers in the church are not disappearing through your ongoing hard work and devotion. You are the great mission-doers of the kingdom of God. Perhaps you will have to do that for a while after you are married. The wives may bear the toil of faith so that the husbands can quickly fulfill the role of Christ in the home.

In summary, the roles of men and women in dating are flexible. The sisters would expect to be spiritually supplied and cared for. But if not, I hope they will urge and nurture the brothers with the heart of Christ. However, the roles of husband and wife should be fixed as in Ephesians 5:22-25 after marriage. It cannot happen all at once, so I hope that the wives will build up and encourage their husbands to do so gradually.

When husbands see such a wife's hard work and dedication, they must be alert and more obedient to the word of Christ! In this way, they must fulfill the ultimate purpose of marriage that the Lord has instituted on this earth. Through the covenant relationship between husband and wife, I pray that we can testify to the world the mystical union of Christ and the church.

Community-Oriented Dating

We are beings who love each other with the love of God because the love within us will someday hit the limit. The same is true in dating. In the early stages of dating, couples will have a spark of love just by looking at each other because of the strong hormone secretion. But when the hormone influence falls, you need the power of love poured out from above.

That love poured out through the Holy Spirit is "community-oriented." This is because the very essence of God is love, and the Triune God pours out that love by forming "a mutual loving community in love."[60] Therefore, our love experienced with His love must also be community-oriented.

When we say that our love should be community-oriented, it means that there is the self who loves first and there is the object of love. That is why the Triune God can be the love in its essence from eternity. It is because the Trinity loves one another even in the absence of us, the object of love. The Trinity is revealed as "One God" despite having three distinct Persons because of "love" that makes them share one essence (substance). This is the heart of the Trinity doctrine.

In any case, both the unmarried and the married have a community-oriented love. Why? Because there is I who love, and there is an

---

60) 권혁빈, 『사랑에 이르는 신학』 (서울: 두란노, 2018), 60.

object that I love. It has a structure called "I-You." That is why, as we argued in Chapter 2, love is always relational. The relational structure of "I and you" is not limited to the two and is necessarily directed outward due to the nature of love. It is the same principle that the love of the Triune God does not remain in Him forever but is expressed outwardly to create the world.

Then the love of couples has a community-oriented attribute in itself, and at the same time is directly connected with the community in which the two live. Why? Because, due to the nature of love, the love between the two cannot remain in them. Their love must be expressed externally and interact with the community in various ways.

Therefore, Christian lovers must influence each other within the community. First of all, they need to make an effort to let the love energy of the two flow positively in the community. True love does not stay in the two but is expressed outward. As mentioned in Chapter 1, couples who dream of God's kingdom and aim in the same direction will recognize that their church exists in His great kingdom and that they exist within the church community. In other words, they become convinced that their dating is not just for each other but for the close community and ultimately for the kingdom of God. That is why they strive to make their love energy contribute to the community somehow or other.

Because of the community-oriented nature of love, Christian dating cannot be separated from the community. It also means that they need to be tested and guided by the community. It's a good idea to tell that you're in a dating relationship at an appropriate time unless absolutely compelled. You have to do that even if he/she belongs to another community. In particular, you should share with the minister in charge or leaders in the church at an appropriate level. Not for them to closely monitor you, but to reflect with you and help you. Unless they are thoughtless, they are bound to work together to keep your relationship going well.

In the field of ministry, I hope that our young Christians can do well in dating. In particular, I wish that many sound and exemplary couples will be born in the same community. But couples don't seem to start out within the same community. Maybe it's because they are so used to each other that especially the brothers in a community don't seem to be "men" in the sisters' eyes. Maybe it means that sisters don't want to see them as men because they think they're boring.

In any case, it is essential to remember that Christian dating is not just an interaction between a couple. They continue to influence and be influenced in their communities. Therefore, they must be aware that all are one body of Christ. You need to know that if your relationship with him/her becomes ill or goes wrong, the whole community is negatively affected. On the other hand, if your relationship with him/her continues beautifully, a good influence flows in the community. Please remember that the church stands amid the kingdom of God, and your dating takes place within the church.

Don't Be Afraid to Break Up!

During dating counseling, I often see some people worried about one thing: "I've just started dating, but I'm worried about what will happen if I break up." When beginning to date, they worry about breaking up. Some young people put the brakes on their dating to avoid becoming close too quickly. It means that they want to keep their relationship for a long time.

Today's dating customs don't seem to know how to break up respectfully. They try to start dating anyway but seem to be not very good at breaking up naturally. There are even cases where dating violence or extreme events are not controlled because of breakups. Such people have the extreme compulsion that dating must continue according to their own will without thinking of the possibility of breaking up.

This is not just a problem for non-Christian lovers. There was a similar case among the church couples I consulted with. One day, the brother received a breakup notice from his girlfriend, but he could not accept it. So he waited in every place she would go, or even waited in front of her house until she came home. The brother's terrifying obsession even continued for months.

One day, I comforted the scared sister and accompanied her to her house. Very tenaciously, the brother was waiting in front of the house that night too. Then she fainted, which surprised me as well as him.

I hurriedly carried her on my back and brought her home. I still can't forget the episode of that day.

Even if you are a Christian couple, this situation can happen if you do not prepare for a breakup respectfully. You need to know the characteristics of people who do not accept a breakup. They are often caught up in tremendous self-loving. These people love their struggling hearts and feelings more than their lovers' state of mind. They should listen to the reason why lovers are having a hard time continuing the relationship. Still, they have the characteristic of repeating their words over and over again. This would be their desperate struggle, saying, "Please, consider my aching heart and emotions."

Usually, such people have a fundamental problem in their relationship with God. Although they say they worship and love God, in reality, they may be loving their own heart toward God. (This does not mean that they have not been saved.) If we analyze their insides, there is a "strong conviction" that God will always listen to them, which is an extreme compulsion that He must do so. As argued in Chapter 4, such a psychological state is also expressed by them because loving God and loving mate are inseparable.

We should understand what love is. To love him/her means to risk everything for him/her. And to love him/her means to embrace all the hurt and pain caused by him/her, even if it is a breakup notice.

In this context, the most painful "breakup" in human history took place on the hill of Golgotha. God forsook Jesus, who loved Him perfectly, on the cross.

My God, my God, why have you forsaken me? (Matt. 27:46; Mark 15:34)

This is the painful cry of Jesus who suffered a "breakup." He knew from the beginning that He would be abandoned by God. It means that while He was on this earth, He loved God perfectly, and yet He had to suffer such a painful "breakup" for the sake of the whole world!

What would have happened if Jesus loved His heart and His feelings more than God's? Then God's plan of salvation for the whole world would have ended in failure. Ironically, the painful and terrifying "breakup" He suffered has brought salvation and peace to humankind.

Likewise, a breakup between lovers does not only leave scars and pain for each other. Above all, it is a golden opportunity to meditate on the sublime "breakup" of the cross with all five senses. What kind of nonsense does this sound like? Even our breakup should be used as material to meditate on His heart and the cross! We sinners have the immaturity to empathize with each other only if we are in a similar situation. A breakup is the best experience, which makes us realize that we can be abandoned by the loved one just like Jesus on the cross. The emotional state of being abandoned and suffered by him/her is similar to that of Him on the cross.

I dare to ask the lovers who have received a breakup notice. I hope you can silently accept the breakup with him/her while meditating on the cross! The current breakup creates an opportunity for another date. Although it is heartbreaking, your breakup provides a dating opportunity with another person. In the grand context of God's kingdom, even your breakup will one day contribute to that kingdom.

After breaking up with my "first love," I thought the sky was falling. After receiving the breakup notice, I couldn't accept it. So I continued to visit her for a while. I waited for several hours in front of her workplace to meet her at the end of the day, but I immediately turned back at her words, "I have to go out with fellow workers."

One day, I succumbed to the love of the cross, came to my senses, and sent a letter to her. It was not a letter to start over but a message to sincerely pray for a future spouse in Christ. I sent my determination to "love" her and be together as a partner for the kingdom of God, just no longer in a dating relationship.

Surprisingly, she keeps in touch and has remained a partner of faith until now. We pray for each other's spouse and family, and above all, we are cooperating in many ways for the kingdom of God. She is currently praying for the missionary work that my family is preparing for financially and spiritually. Looking back now, more than 20 years later since then, the breakup at that time was a temporary pain for missions and the expansion of God's kingdom.

I ask young people who are about to break up: "Please do not be too heartbroken or afraid of!" When you break up, God will also be heartbroken and watch over you because He had also experienced a "breakup." I hope you don't miss God's grand plan for you due to being engrossed in your breakup. In the grand context of the kingdom of God, there is no eternal breakup or eternal pain. There is only a "temporary breakup" in order to enjoy eternal delight together in Christ.

 ## Summary and Advice on Dating

Now the next chapter will be about marriage. Before that, I would like to end with a brief summary and practical advice related to dating. The readers can summarize and organize even those not listed below in their own language from this book.

1. The beginning of dating occurs in various ways. It would be nice to have the same heart together, dreaming of the kingdom of God. But in reality, we frequently start by being drawn to a simple liking or sexual attraction. Don't limit yourself to one thing; keep all possibilities open. When someone proposes a blind date, don't ask anything other than faith and meet first.

2. If you see a potential person, check his/her faith first. If he/

she ever seems to have infirm faith, you have to decide. Whether to nurture him/her spiritually while dating, if you're not confident about that, you'd better just give up. In particular, it is better for sisters not to expect spiritual supply unless the brother will become a minister.

3. When dating begins, you should get to know each other deeply in various aspects (faith, daily life, relationship, etc.). Keep in mind that the deeper the physical touch, the more difficult it is to get to know each other properly. Use appropriate touch, but set an uncompromising point before God by talking to each other.

4. You must immediately repent if you crossed the marginal line (kiss, sexual intercourse) before marriage. Public confession of sins is not recommended. Instead, go to your pastor, parents, or seniors of faith to inform them of the situation, have a time of repentance in their sight, and promise not to repeat it. And according to the principle of the Word, the two must be married (Ex. 22:16; Deut. 22:29).

5. Remember that the more you control your sexual arousal, the richer your newly-married life will be. Moreover, you have to try hard to develop such restraint when dating so that you can control the sexual attraction toward another person after marriage. Even if we get married, our sexual desires are lurking in the sinful nature of wanting to be expressed to others.

6. Unless absolutely compelled, you should share the fact about dating with the community. A dating that does not interact with the community eventually causes a couple to focus only on each other. In particular, objective verification of their faith and character becomes impossible. The reason for wanting to secretly date is simple: no one can interfere in their dating.

7. During dating, you must go through the process of confirming and coordinating each other's missions. Of course, you don't have to give up on dating just because you do not discover your mission yet. Even in the process of dating, you can dream of God's kingdom together and discover a mission as much as you want. Usually, if either party has a clear mission, they can continue a rich dating.

8. Above all else, you two should strive to love God more together. Do not fall into the "division-allotment concept" but continue your faith training in such a way that the more you love each other, the more you love God. Listen to and imitate practical advice from married people who have had beautiful dating.

9. If the relationship deepens and you consider getting married, you must share it with your parents. Remember that marriage is not a union between individuals, but families and families. Unless there is a special reason, you should reconsider marriage that your parents

are overly opposed to. Or you have to convince parents to accept and bless their children's marriage.

10. Don't be afraid to break up in dating. No matter how much you love each other, if your missions are not coordinated, and your temperament or thoughts continue to clash, you can break up. However, before you break up, take some time and prepare for a "respectful breakup." If possible, promise to pray for each other's future spouses and try to remain partners for the kingdom of God.

11. If you miss the marriageable age or live single for other reasons, there is no need to become diffident. Although we should put our utmost effort into dating and marriage, there are cases where, like the apostle Paul, we live alone and contribute greatly to God's kingdom and the church. You must not fall into the absolutes of dating and marriage. Marriage and "marriageism" are different.

1. What do you think is the reason why it is difficult to find a mate in the church? If there may be analyses different from the author's, please share them.

2. Are you dating a non-Christian, or do you have any desire to date so in the future? Please share honestly what the reason is.

3. Do you think you have a high standard for the opposite sex? Or do you think it is average or rather low? Do others agree with it?

4. If you are currently dating, what roles do you and he/she play, respectively? Who has spiritual leadership, and what direction do you want to go in the future?

5. Are dating couples giving and receiving positive influences on the community? Or is there an atmosphere where people should never interfere in their dating?

6. Have you ever experienced a breakup? Please share your mind and situation at that time and how you overcame it.

Chapter
7.

Marriage and Married Life

It is often said that first love lasts a lifetime. There is a song called "A Man's First Love Goes To The Grave,"[61] although it is a bit old. The lyrics of this song even say, "You have always been the standard of love." That is to say, "first love" influences a man enormously.

This is the concept of first love that non-Christians say and feel. Although we may share some attributes of love with them, we cannot fully accept their concept of love. The concept of first love must also be derived from the Bible.

Interestingly, the expression "first love" appears in Revelation 2:4.

Nevertheless I have *this* against you, that you have left your first love. (NKJV)

This is the Lord's warning to the church in Ephesus. The Lord is aware of their tremendous hard work, perseverance, and zeal, but they do not have their first love for the Lord. It doesn't mean that the relationship with the Lord has been cut off, but it means that they are losing the love they had for the Lord at first. No matter how hard they work, persevere, and show zeal, if they don't love the Lord as they did

---

61) This is an English translation. The original Korean title is "남자의 첫사랑은 무덤까지 간다." This song is included in *Cheerful Sensibility*, released in June 2007 by male band FT Island. See this website: https://vibe.naver.com/track/800442 (accessed January 8, 2022).

at first, then all of those really aren't for the Lord!

It also leads to a loss of love for neighbors. As covered in Chapter 4, the Bible consistently teaches that loving God and loving neighbor are inseparable. If you lose your first love for the Lord, your love for your neighbor will also change. Why? Because all love flows out of our relationship with God.

We can meditate on another aspect of the meaning in this verse. The point is that when the Lord begins a relationship with us and pours out His love, He describes it as "first love." Of course, the contextual meaning of first love is the same as already described. However, the meaning of the commonly used phrase "Jesus, my first love" can be extracted from this verse.

As some scholar has pointed out, "your first love" of Revelation 2:4 can be said to be "'the love you had at first,' that is, shortly after their conversion."[62] Here, I would like to pay attention to the expression "shortly after their conversion." Conversion is our response to the regeneration (to be born again) caused by the Holy Spirit. It means starting an irrevocable covenant relationship with God. Simply put, after we "are married" to Christ, we recognize it and respond practically for the first time. Then the love with Him at this point is called "first love."

If so, please think about it. First love is based on the covenant with

---

62) Grant R. Osborne, *Revelation*, BECNT (Grand Rapids, MI: Baker Academic, 2002), 115.

Him. Now it has become the love we have for Him for the first time on the premise of an irrevocable relationship. Truly, from our point of view, it is very sorry to put the modifier "first" in front of love. Although it is a first for Him, it is not for us. Before we met Him, we were in an impure "love" with Satan, "the prince of the power of the air" (Eph. 2:2).

Nevertheless, we must say, "The Lord is our first love!" when covenant-based love begins. Why? Because the love with Him in the Bible is a covenant love that cannot be broken, and we have this love with the Lord for the first time. Also, this covenant love is the first love and the last love. This is because there is no possibility to be broken, and the object of love does not change.

Now we should apply the relationship between Christ and the church in a corresponding way. As I have already mentioned several times, marriage is the "great mystery" that reveals the mystical union with Him. According to that principle, the Christian couple's concept of first love must be corrected. The concept of first love involves a covenant with an object, namely, an irrevocable relationship.

So, who is the first love of Christian lovers? The very person they get married to is their first love. This is because marriage is the moment when covenant love begins. Marriage is a covenant that can never be broken because God has joined the two together. That is why it is fundamentally different from dating. The physical attraction may be much more intense during dating. Still, regardless of the attraction, the real union lies in marriage.

Strictly speaking, the "love" of couples before marriage is not yet love. Why? Because covenant love begins from the moment when they get married. The "love" that couples enjoy before marriage is deep intimacy, accompanied by sexual attraction. In this book, for conventional reasons, emotional intimacy between unmarried lovers is simply expressed as "love." With this in mind, you will understand the contents more clearly if you look back at the previous parts.

So I can tell confidently: My current wife is my first love! Why? Because I had never had a covenant love before, and I first started that love with my wife in July 2005. In this context, the sisters I dated before are not the object of love, which I am sorry to say. Even the love I enjoyed with her before marriage is not a covenant love. This is because such love begins from the moment when we get married, whom God has joined together as "one flesh." In this context, Christians are not marrying because they love, but they are marrying in order to love. I will close with a diagram table to help you understand at a glance.

 ## Three Principles of Covenant Marriage

Marriage is a covenant that cannot be broken. It does not refer to the reality of marriage but to the nature of marriage that God

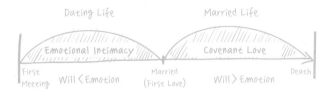

Emotional Intimacy vs. Covenant Love

originally intended. The covenant of marriage based on the covenant relationship with God is "not temporary, but eternal."[63] It means that the covenant cannot be irrevocable until the substance arrives. This is because God intended the relationship between Christ and the church to be witnessed through the covenant relationship of husband and wife (Eph. 5:31-32).

There are three principles in this marriage, the covenant. Let's go back to Genesis 2:24 (NKJV) mentioned in Chapter 1.

Therefore a man shall leave his father and mother and be joined to his wife, and they shall become one flesh.

Three principles of covenant marriage are contained in this one short verse. The first is "to leave." The first principle is that a man leaves his parents, and this implies at the same time that a woman

★

63) 프레드 로워리, 『결혼은 하나님과 맺은 언약입니다』, 임종원 옮김 (서울: 미션월드 라이브러리, 2003), 97.

leaves her parents. It doesn't mean that you should not live in the same house with your parents or that you should cut off your relationship with your parents. But it means that you should become independent from the emotional bond or intimacy formed with your parents. Simply put, your number one priority is a husband or wife.

It seems that more and more newlyweds are not following the first principle well. When they start their married life, the husband and wife don't seem to think that they are now standing before God separately from their parents as the smallest unit of the family. In many cases, they are still emotionally dependent on their parents.

Here is a story of a young couple who I consulted. One day, a sister who was in the period of consideration for divorce came to me. During the marriage of five years, her husband asked his mother for help whenever problems occurred. So she reproached him for his immature behaviors. Her mother-in-law was unilaterally covering up her son, even forcing him to divorce his wife. Ironically, the mother-in-law was a senior deaconess in the church.

There may be various problems between them. In my view, although the husband is living with his wife physically, he is still bound to his parents emotionally. To make matters worse, his mother stirs it up even more, far from scolding her son. To borrow a psychological term, the husband is still in "emotional fusion" with his mother. Since their emotions are inseparable and bound together, they feel and react to everything that happens on one side as if it were their own. This is a phenomenon in which the love between parents and children is distorted.

The covenant of marriage is an exclusive relationship only between husband and wife. It must be "exclusive faithfulness" towards your spouse above any other object. Even parents cannot have control over their relationship except for proper advice. Parents must never think of their children's divorcing! It is a terrible sin that breaks the covenant joined together by God. Parents and children should never forget that the covenant between husband and wife premises "to leave" from the parents.

Next, the second principle of covenant marriage is "to unite." It follows as a result of the first principle ("to leave"). According to the expression of Genesis 2:24 (NKJV), husband and wife "are joined" to each other. The Hebrew verb *dabaq* (דבק) for "to join" means to solder two metal pieces and stick them together.[64] They are in a state where they cannot be separated under any external pressure. Likewise, husband and wife must now remember that they will never be separated from each other no matter what the circumstances. In particular, the husband must resolve firmly not to be separated from her wife under any circumstances.

Based on this principle, married couples should not live apart from

64) Ray Ortlund, *Marriage and the Mystery of the Gospel,* ed. Dane C. Ortlund and Miles Van Pelt, Short Studies in Biblical Theology (Wheaton, IL: Crossway, 2016), 30.

each other. Except for temporary unavoidable cases, husband and wife must stay together. Here is my shameful confession. When I was a seminary student, my church and home were far away. My church was in Seoul, my house was in Daegu, and I was busy studying at the seminary in Cheonan. So I couldn't even be with my wife on weekends.

Once every two months, I would go home to see my newborn first baby and wife. I could not move to Seoul for some reason. The fact that my house was far away negatively affected my ministry too. I even felt the church sisters more familiar for a while. That is why male ministers must stick with their wives to protect themselves and the church. Even in a married state, if you ignore the principle of covenant marriage and behave according to your thoughts, you may fall into serious sins.

Finally, the third principle of covenant marriage is "to become one flesh." It is the inevitable consequence of the second principle ("to unite"). The word *one* is the same meaning as the word *one* from "the Triune God is *one*," and the word *flesh* "suggests the transient mortality of this life."[65] Therefore, to become one flesh means that until the day the married couple dies on this earth, their lives become one, and they fully share each other's lives. In other words, when one hurts, the other suffers as well, and when the other is happy, one rejoices.

---

*

65) Ibid.

Sexual intercourse between husband and wife is a means of outwardly demonstrating this "one flesh." It is God's gift allowed for "married couples," not unmarried, to vividly recognize that they are one flesh with their five senses. So the third principle of covenant marriage ("to become one flesh") includes the sexual intercourse between husband and wife. In particular, this is the act of expressing the second principle (i.e., the union) with the whole body. It is very beautiful in God's sight if it is not a distorted expression of sexual desire.

These three principles of covenant marriage must now manifest their ultimate substance. Let's put them in other words as the relationship between Christ and the church. We have "left" the world, have been "united" with Christ, and become "one flesh" with Him, including His believers. According to the first principle, we are beings who have experienced a spiritual leaving from the world. In Paul's words, "by whom [Christ] the world has been crucified to me, and I to the world" (Gal. 6:14, NKJV). We are completely departed from the dominance of the world, and this is our covenant status.

According to the second principle, we are "united" with Christ. It is the inevitable result of leaving from the world. "Neither death nor life, nor angels nor rulers, . . . nor anything else in all creation, will be able to separate us from the love of God in Christ Jesus our Lord" (Rom. 8:38-39). This means an unbreakable relationship that will last forever. The One who initiated this union guarantees it forever. He even sealed us as His own and gave the Holy Spirit into our hearts as a guarantee (2 Cor. 1:22).

According to the third and final principle, we have become "one flesh" with Christ. It is the result of an unbreakable union. Christ, the Bridegroom, loves us, His bride (the church), most deeply and secretly. "As the bridegroom rejoices over the bride, so shall your God rejoice over you" (Isa. 62:5). We are one body with Himself, including His saints in His active and perfect love.

Are we really enjoying the spiritual dimension of covenant marriage? Checking this is surprisingly simple. Please remember the principle that loving God and loving mate cannot be separated. If you don't "leave" your parents or end your emotional relationship with your ex, you are just as unfaithful to God as to your spouse. I want you to recall the convergence of love and the convergence of sin discussed in Chapter 4. These are the principles that love or crime toward your spouse results in love or crime toward God.

The same is true of "union" and "one flesh," which are the inevitable results of the first principle. The substance of union and one flesh with Christ is eternal and unchanging, but enjoying it in our daily lives is another matter. This can also be checked through the relationship with your spouse. That is to say, if you do not enjoy emotional and sexual intimacy with your spouse except for special cases, it is almost inevitable that you will not be able to enjoy spiritual intimacy with the Lord. Why? Because the relationship between Christ and the church (i.e., us) is revealed through the relationship between husband

and wife. The relationship between the two should not be considered separately for even a moment.

I'm really ashamed of myself. I have often mistakenly believed that even though I have relationship troubles with my wife, my love for the Lord has not changed. Unless there is a special case, the state in which I love my spouse is the current state of loving God. Isn't it really terrific? God intended our marriage in that way to reveal the mystical union of Christ and the church (i.e., loving God = loving spouse). If so, are married people, including me, really aware of such principles in their marriages?

 ## Marriage Is Based on God!

I have ever officiated the wedding of a bride and groom. A sermon that I preached at the wedding has been added to the appendix of this book. All the weddings bring beauty and impression to the officiant and the guests present. I didn't realize it very much when I attended as a guest, but when I stood as the officiant in front of the bride and groom and guests, I could vividly feel God's heart for His "bride" (the church).

Seeing the bride's father holding her hand enters with the background of colorful lights, the first human wedding ceremony comes to mind reflexively. It overlaps exquisitely with the scene in which

God leads Eve to Adam after making her from Adam's rib. And as the bride's Father and "Officiant," God joins together the two as a married couple. At this point, Adam is filled with the joy of covenant marriage and begins to sing humankind's first nuptial song. "This at last is bone of my bones and flesh of my flesh; she shall be called Woman, because she was taken out of Man" (Gen. 2:23). The next verse tells about the institution of marriage. "Therefore a man shall leave his father and mother and be joined to his wife, and they shall become one flesh" (Gen. 2:24, NKJV).

As you can see, in the first wedding ceremony of humankind, God Himself officiated and joined the two together. Therefore, the basis of their covenant marriage lies in God. This principle that "the basis of covenant marriage is God Himself" has not changed ever. It is because the eternal attribute of the covenant belongs to God.

We need to examine where the bride and groom base their marriage upon. We must not thoughtlessly accept today's marriage culture, which increasingly refuses an officiant. Even if those of the world are like that, we must ordain a legal officiant who bases our covenant marriage on God. This is because he plays the role of joining together the bride and groom on behalf of the first Officiant.

The moment when the marriage takes place lies in the officiant's pronouncement. In other words, marriage is done from the moment he pronounces publicly in front of the guests and the church, saying, "I pronounce you husband and wife in the name of the Father, the

Son, and the Holy Spirit." This is because, as in the first wedding of humankind, the basis of covenant marriage lies in the Triune God. Since the name refers to existence, to pronounce in the name of the Triune God is to "bet on God's existence" to confirm the marriage as a covenant. Therefore, the covenant marriage cannot be broken unless the Triune God is divided.

In this regard, practical problems sometimes occur in the church. If the groom or bride's family does not believe in the Lord, they do not want a pastor as an officiant. They actually ordain an ordinary person who is not a pastor. It would be best for the bride and groom to convince both parents with a firmer attitude, but this is not always possible in reality.

What should we do in this case? There was such a case in the young adult department I was in charge of. The groom's family stubbornly opposed the Christian wedding. So, a week before the wedding, the ministers prepared a nuptial song and invited the bride and groom and the bride's parents. We held the "mini wedding" that the senior pastor officiated. Because the Christian bride and groom's covenant marriage is based on the name of the Triune God, under no circumstances could we give up the pronouncement in His name.

Non-Christians cannot understand our attitude. Since they do not believe in the Triune God, we do not need to be overly sensitive to their blame. They base their marriage on marriage registration. Of course, they make a vow in front of the guests during the wedding, but the vow does not act as a final basis in their mind. We, too, must register our marriage in the sense of respecting social law in order to share the legal basis for marriage with them.

Even so, we must know exactly. Christian bride and groom's marriage is based on the pronouncement in the name of the Triune God. To add to that, the marriage registration is an outward sign that seals it. This can be compared to baptism, the seal of our faith. That is to say, just as baptism is a public seal of spiritual marriage (union) with Christ, marriage registration is a social confirmation of the bride and groom's marriage.

Covenant, the Power That Causes the Duty of Love

It seems that more and more married people hate the word *duty*. They think of living by duty as bondage and even long for "freedom." This is due to a misunderstanding of the word *duty*. It is not a duty as bondage but a duty of love based on the covenant. Simply put, it is a duty that comes from loving the spouse with whom you have made a covenant.

But what if you no longer love your spouse? What if the two components (will and emotion) of love have already been extinguished within you? Then should we endure day by day degenerating into a duty of bondage rather than a duty of love?

The love between husband and wife is based on the covenant of marriage. Because of the covenant's nature that cannot be broken, their love should not change. It's not just about the "emotion" of love, and even the "will" to love often changes. The attributes of covenant love are unchanging, but married love is very variable in reality. There are cases where only their bodies are in the same house, but their love no longer exists. My parents lived like that and eventually got divorced when I was young.

So, what sustains marriage is not the love between husband and wife. Instead, the covenant of marriage sustains their love. The covenant is a fence that protects love. While you don't love your spouse, you must fulfill your duty because of that covenant. You must do so unless you break the covenant.

That is why we must not continue to neglect the loss of our love. If you keep trying to find the strength to love your spouse within yourself, you will come to a point where it is no longer possible. Therefore, such strength must come from the Lord. Since loving your spouse and loving the Lord are inseparable, your love for the Lord is almost gone if you get to that point.

What should we do in this case? We must seek His grace to pour out His unfailing love toward us. We need to remember that even though my love for Him may change, His love for me will not change forever. We are sinners who often break marital covenants.[66] Still, we must believe that our Bridegroom never breaks the covenant He made with us and pours out eternal love "based on that covenant."

Marriage is a way to testify to the relationship between Christ and the church. But we must always realize that even it is possible through God's grace. Christian couples need to break free from the illusion that their love will last forever. Then they must continue to rely on God, who keeps His unchanging covenant of love for them. It means to place the source of marital love in His grace from above.

Here is my shameful confession. I often feel that love for my wife is variable. Obviously, on the day of the wedding, I made a vow, *"In the name of God, I, Ryul Kwon, take you, Mi-Ae Son, to be my wife, to have and to hold from this day forward, for better, for worse, for richer, for poorer, in sickness and in health, to love and to cherish, until we are parted by death. This is my solemn vow."* [67] At first, I remembered this vow and kept it with all my might, but I showed a lack of fidelity to it as time passed. I wanted my feelings and emotions to be respected before my wife's position. Also, I often showed my sinful nature of subtly insisting on my thoughts while raising our children.

Even in this state, I "believed" that my love for God was the same. Until the Holy Spirit exposed my misunderstanding, I thought it would be possible to love God regardless of my wife. At this point, I

★

66) I did not deal with the issue of divorce in detail because it seemed outside the nature of this book. For the issue of divorce and remarriage of saints, please refer to the Westminster Confession of Faith, Chapter 24, "Marriage and Divorce."

67) I cited the vow statement on this site: https://texasformarriage.org/6-best-traditional-protestant-wedding-vows (accessed January 8, 2022).

failed to testify to the mystical union of Christ and the church. Christ wants my marriage to testify to the way He loves the church, but I didn't love my wife the same way He does. The covenant of marriage should strengthen the duty of love. But I neglected the duty rather because the covenant could not be broken. This is blasphemy against the covenant. Furthermore, it is blasphemy against God who has instituted the covenant of marriage.

I realized that I was a sinner too, and I had no choice but to rely on God's grace and mercy. As I repeat, I am not writing this book since I am faithful to "theology of dating" and "theology of marriage." The content of this book includes many episodes of my failed dating and married life. Referring to them, I share with my readers what I have learned, relying on the Lord's grace. Therefore, the content of this book has experiential characteristics.

Anyway, the covenant is the power that causes the duty of love! It is a fence that protects the married even when their love is almost gone. Also, it is a power to reawaken the duty of love towards the spouse, as in my case. This covenant is based on the covenant relationship of Christ and the church in the Holy Spirit, and it originates from God. Therefore, everything in our marriage and our life of faith comes from the Triune God.

We must ultimately realize the heart of God, who is faithful to the covenant. Husbands and wives must embody in their marriage His words, "I will not violate my covenant or alter the word that went forth from my lips" (Ps. 89:34). We don't do our duty with the mind of being tied to our spouse. But we are willing to do our duty because we love our spouse based on the covenant.

Childbirth and Nurture

Many years ago, I got an unexpected question from my college friend. His wife was weak and had a hard time giving birth, so raising a baby made her even harder. He asked:

> Jonathan, animals' babies grow up in a few months or years after birth. Why does it take humans' babies so long? Please pray to God and let me know the answer.

I also had the first child at that time, so I often thought that way. After receiving his question and praying for a while, I suddenly realized something. So I contacted my friend again.

> I have been praying to God for your question. I think God wants us to realize His heart through it, and He wants us as parents to know how much hard work and patience He puts in until He adopts a soul in Christ and stands him fully before Him.

This conversation with the friend remained in my memory ten years later. In this way, God wants us to realize another aspect of His heart through marriage. As it is often said, giving birth to children is a "creation mandate," and raising children is a "redemption mandate." Creation and redemption are the co-work of the Triune God for us. We, who were created in God's image, carry out God's work, especially through marriage. Also, just as the Trinity did not work independently, husbands and wives in His image must jointly bear the creation mandate (childbirth) and redemption mandate (nurture).

Childbirth, which is a creation mandate for married couples, is the work that forms the foundation of God's kingdom and the church. The prophet Malachi urged the Israelites to be faithful to the covenant and revealed God's heart that "He seeks godly offspring" through marriage (Mal. 2:15, NKJV). The godly descendants who believe in God are the members of God's kingdom and the church. It begins with believers marrying and producing many covenant people.

Of course, I know that there are many practical problems. The social structure is becoming increasingly difficult for newlyweds to give birth as much as they like. It is difficult for Christian couples to carry out God's creation mandate. Given the nature of the world that does not know God, it may be a "natural" phenomenon.

So, even when it comes to childbirth, a decision of faith is required. We must be able to view childbirth in the context of the kingdom of God and the fulfillment of His vision. The Lord Himself accomplishes the kingdom of God, but He also uses childbirth as a means of achieving that work. He leads the world's people to be converted and enter the kingdom of God. Still, God primarily wants to get godly descendants through the childbirth of the saints. Therefore, please do not forsake the creation mandate because of practical difficulties, but focus on childbearing according to the measure of your faith.

This creation mandate (childbirth) also leads to a redemption mandate (nurture). It is as if God redeemed the fallen world by the power of the Holy Spirit in Christ. Christian parents should raise their children in order to know God experientially based on the blessings of the covenant. It means that we should lead them to possess the knowledge of "knowing God," not "knowing about God."

I often realize through raising children God's heart to redeem the world. This is because my children look like me standing before God. I have three sons. In fact, most of the child-raising is done by my wife. So I don't have the right to speak honorably about it. Nevertheless, thanks to the mercy of the Lord, I continue to exhort my readers.

Child-raising or nurture is a redemption mandate because we must pass on the knowledge of God based on the gospel to our children. Going out into the world, preaching the gospel to unbelievers, and converting them should not be only considered a redemption mandate. Although those are essential and emphasized in the New Testament, nurturing the children of the covenant is very important in the whole of the Old and New Testaments.

We cannot build the kingdom of God and the church only through childbirth (creation mandate). It would be possible if sin did not enter the world. However, due to the nature of the world against God, His kingdom must be accomplished in a way that kills sin through nurture (redemption mandate). Therefore, the power of the cross and resurrection of Christ must take over the daily lives of our children.

Finally, as parents, we must remember that childbirth and nurture are also a means of revealing the relationship between Christ and the church. Just as Christ loves the church and the church is moved by His love and gives birth to another convert, married couples also love each other and give birth to and nurture children of faith. As mentioned in the previous chapter, this is because of the nature of love that overflows outward. It is the same principle as if the love of the Triune God overflowed so that the work of creation and redemption was accomplished.

1. Do you think that the so-called "first love" lasts a lifetime? If you think so, what memories or atmosphere with him/her hold you like that?

2. Explain the three principles of covenant marriage in your own language once again.

3. If you are considering getting married to the person you are now dating, please share in detail how you would like to prepare for the wedding.

4. When you have a hard time loving your spouse during the marriage, how would you like to overcome your condition?

5. If you marry your lover in the future, from what perspective do you want to treat childbirth and nurture? In particular, how many children do you plan to have, and how would you like to raise them?

Dreaming the Conversion of
Christian Dating

Now I would like to summarize the gist of this book. As you know, except for Chapter 7, it is all about Christian "dating." Of course, I often mentioned general things about marriage to compare it with the attributes of dating. I am confident that dating and marriage are closely related to the daily life of the kingdom of God. That is, dating and marriage are aiming for His kingdom that will be consummated in the future, and simultaneously are a part of His kingdom that has already come.

So I approached it quite differently from the usual books about dating and marriage. There are many similar books about marriage because it is treated in the Bible. But among the books about Christian dating, this book might seem a bit unique. Again, the fundamental desires of Christian young adults must be directed toward the kingdom of God and His vision! Because of such a conviction, I have developed "a theology of dating" based on the Bible and doctrine. Young people need to be trained to yield the most challenging dating issue to God's sovereignty. I hope that this book will be put to practical use.

As a pastor, I am dreaming of actual conversion of Christian dating. I want to strongly ask the Christian lovers of this age through my clumsy dating experience and the married life I am still learning. I hope you remember that Christian dating is the most significant area distinguishing between you and the world in your youth. I pray you can reject the thought outright, "I'm going to get married anyway, so I'll date in the world's way." Please remember that beautiful dating in Christ is the "worship" in your youth that God is so pleased with.

Finally, I will summarize the differences between dating and marriage in four sentences. Even if you do not agree with some parts, please accept them as positively as possible.

1. Dating is the immature stage of being "driven" by the emotional side of love,
   Marriage is a more mature stage of being "dedicated" to the volitional (will-related) side of love.

2. Dating is the process of confirming and coordinating each other's missions for marriage,
   Marriage is a life's journey of passionately loving each other for

God's vision.

3. Dating is the process of preparing and training for love,
   Marriage is the best training ground for seeking and realizing covenant love.

4. Dating is a partial shadow of marriage,
   Marriage is a "complete" shadow of mystical union with Christ.

A Wedding Ceremony Sermon

"This Is a Great Mystery!"

Dearly Beloved, today we are here with the bride and groom who are about to take their wedding vows. Soon, the two will be officially married in the presence of God and many witnesses. This moment will remain the most moving memory for these two. This is because after living different lives for at least 35 years, they met each other in God's providence and are about to become one flesh.

As a pastor, I would like to share with you for a moment about the holy and precious marriage that God has instituted. The marriage of saints is a solemn moment when covenant love begins. Unlike the world, we value the marriage of a man and a woman according to God's principle of creation. Marriage of brother and sister who believe in Jesus does not simply mean that one person and one person meet and live together. As you can see from the sermon title, there is a great mystery hidden in the marriage of saints.

As you know, God created Adam to work and keep the Garden of Eden (Gen. 2:15). Then God said: "It is not good that the man should be alone; I will make him a helper fit for him" (2:18). To say that it is not good for the man to live alone does not mean that he is lonely just because he is alone. It means that it is not good to alone carry out the mission God has given to Adam. That is why God gave a gift (Eve) to Adam as a "helper."

After God put Adam into a deep sleep and made a woman, He brought her to Adam (2:22). This is humankind's first wedding, and God is like the bride's father leading his daughter to the groom. In the first wedding ceremony, God became the Parent and Officiant and, at the same time, officiated the wedding of Adam and Eve.

Our situation now reproduces what it was like back then. Of course, as a pastor, I officiate, but now the genuine Officiant of the bride and groom is the Lord God. Marriage is a kind of "covenant" made before God. The Lord is the witness of this covenant marriage and joins together the bride and groom. No one can separate the bride and groom now because God has joined them together (Mark 10:9). For this fact, you and I are here as guests and witnesses.

Looking at verse 31 in the text, there are three principles of covenant marriage. The first is that a man leaves his parents. The bride and groom will now leave their parents. This means being emotionally, relationally, and socially independent. So far, they have been obedient and protected by their parents, but the bride and groom have to shape their own lives from now on. In particular, it means that the groom has left his parents and must put the bride as the top priority.

The second is that the two are joined to each other. The Hebrew word *dabaq* (Gen. 2:24) for "to join" means to solder two metal pieces and stick them together (Isa. 41:7). They are in a state where they cannot be separated under any external pressure. Likewise, the bride and groom must now remember that they will never be separated from each other no matter what the circumstances. In particular, the groom must resolve firmly not to be separated from the bride under any circumstances.

The third and final is that the two become one flesh. The word *one* is the same meaning as the word *one* from "the Triune God is *one,*" and the word *flesh* refers to a temporary life on this earth. Therefore, becoming one flesh means that until the day the married couple dies on this earth, their lives become one, and they fully share each other's lives. In other words, when one hurts, the other suffers as well, and when the other is happy, one rejoices.

These three are the precious principles contained in covenant marriage. However, the marriage of our saints does not end there. Let's all look at verse 32 together. The apostle Paul refers to the marriage (v. 31; Gen. 2:24), saying, "This is a great mystery" (v. 32). Why would he say, "This is a great mystery?" Because, as it follows, the marriage of saints speaks concerning "Christ and the church."

In other words, this marriage between the bride and groom is not just a brother-sister marriage but ultimately represents the relationship between Christ and the church. That is to say, the groom loves the bride as Christ loves the church, and the bride serves the groom as the church serves Christ.

How does Jesus Christ love us as the church? He loves us to the point of laying down His life on the cross. At this level, I hope the groom will continue to love his bride from today onwards! If the groom truly loves the bride with the love of the cross, perhaps the bride will serve the groom voluntarily. There is no bride in the world who will not budge when the groom loves to the point of laying down his life.

Is this advice too burdensome? Then I'll lower it one level and exhort it with the words of verse 33. Let us read it all together. "Nevertheless let each one of you in particular so love his own wife as himself, and let the wife *see* that she respects *her* husband." The groom just should be able to love his bride at least as much as he loves himself. The bride also should have respect for the groom. This exhortation is directed not only to the bride and groom but also to all guests present.

I am a husband of three sons, but sometimes I do not love my wife as much as I love myself, and I feel how regretful I am at such time. Of course, there are times when she doesn't respect me either. Whenever she does not, I often resent her. But I rather blame myself for not eliciting her voluntary respect. You can experience how challenging the role of a husband would be when you get married.

Anyway, we are gathered here to celebrate the bride and groom's wedding and bless their future. Since we are all one family in Christ, we must continue to work together for the kingdom of God and the church even after this wedding is over. Please pray together so that their holy mission God has given can be fulfilled through the married life that begins today.

Finally, as the officiant, I give another word of encouragement to the bride and groom. I earnestly bless you that you can build a beautiful family of faith in the Lord and love each other unchangingly in any situation. Amen.

Officiant, Pastor Ryul Kwon
Saturday, March 30, 2019

▓ BIBLES

Biblia Hebraica Stuttgartensia. With Werkgroep Informatica, Vrije Universiteit Morphology;
    Bible. O.T. Hebrew. Werkgroep Informatica, Vrije Universiteit. Logos Bible Software, 2006.

Novum Testamentum Graece. Edited by Barbara Aland, Kurt Aland, Johannes Karvidopoulos,
    Carlo M. Martini, and Bruce M. Metzger, 28th ed. Stuttgart: Deutsche Bibelgesellschaft, 2012.

The Holy Bible. English Standard Version. Wheaton, Illinois: Crossway Bibles, 2016.

The Holy Bible. New International Version. Grand Rapids, MI: Zondervan, 2011.

The Holy Bible. New King James Version. Nashville: Thomas Nelson, 1982.

▓ ENGLISH BOOKS

Bauer, Walter. *A Greek-English Lexicon of the New Testament and Other Early Christian Literature.* Revised
    and edited by Frederick William Danker, 3rd. ed. Chicago: The University of Chicago Press, 2000.

Dennis, Lane T. and Wayne Grudem. eds. *ESV Study Bible.* Wheaton, Illinois: Crossway, 2008.

Elliot, Elisabeth. *Passion and Purity: Learning to Bring Your Love Life under Christ's Control.* Grand Rapids,
    MI: Revell, 2021.

Fromm, Erich. *The Art of Loving.* London: Bradford & Dickens, Drayton House. 1956.

Hendriksen, William and Simon J. Kistemaker. *Exposition of Ephesians,* vol. 7, New Testament
    Commentary. Grand Rapids, MI: Baker Book House, 1953-2001.

Lewis, C. S. *The Four Loves.* New York: Harcourt, Brace and Company, 1960.

Lewis, Gordon R. and Bruce A. Demarest. *Integrative Theology, Volume 2: Our Primary Need: Christ's
    Atoning Provisions.* Grand Rapids, MI: Zondervan, 1990.

Myers, Allen C. "kiss," in *The Eerdmans Bible Dictionary.* Grand Rapids, MI: Eerdmans, 1987.

Nolland, John. *The Gospel of Matthew: A Commentary on the Greek Text.* The New International Greek
    Testament Commentary. Grand Rapids, MI: William B. Eerdmans Publishing Company, 2005.

Ortlund, Ray. *Marriage and the Mystery of the Gospel,* ed. Dane C. Ortlund and Miles Van Pelt. Short
    Studies in Biblical Theology. Wheaton, IL: Crossway, 2016.

Osborne, Grant R. *Revelation.* Baker Exegetical Commentary on the New Testament. Grand Rapids, MI:
    Baker Academic, 2002.

Piper, John. *Preparing for Marriage*. Minneapolis, MN: Desiring God, 2018.

_____. *This Momentary Marriage*. Wheaton, Illinois: Crossway Books, 2009.

Saint Augustine of Hippo. *The Confessions of St. Augustine*, V.iv. Translated by E. B. Pusey. Oak Harbor, WA: Logos Research Systems, Inc., 1996.

_____. "On the Trinity," in *St. Augustine: On the Holy Trinity, Doctrinal Treatises, Moral Treatises*, Edited by Philip Schaff. Translated by Arthur West Haddan. vol. 3. *A Select Library of the Nicene and Post-Nicene Fathers of the Christian Church, First Series*. Buffalo, NY: Christian Literature Company, 1887.

Saint-Exupery, Antoine de. *Wind, Sand and Stars*. Translated from the French by Lewis Galantiere. New York: Reynal & Hitchcock, 1939.

Soanes, Catherine and Angus Stevenson, eds. "vision," in *Concise Oxford English Dictionary*. Oxford: Oxford University Press, 2004.

▒ KOREAN BOOKS

권율. 『올인원 십계명』 서울: 세움북스, 2019.

___. 『올인원 주기도문』 서울: 세움북스, 2018.

권혁빈. 『사랑에 이르는 신학』 서울: 두란노, 2018.

김세윤. 『칭의와 성화』 서울: 두란노, 2013.

김정우. 『시편 주석 Ⅱ』 서울: 총신대학교출판부, 2005.

로워리, 프레드. 『결혼은 하나님과 맺은 언약입니다』 임종원 옮김. 서울: 미션월드 라이브러리, 2003.

리고니어 미니스트리. 『개혁주의 스터디 바이블』 김진운, 김찬영, 김태형, 신윤수, 윤석인 옮김. 서울: 부흥과개혁사, 2017.

백금산 편. 『조나단 에드워즈처럼 살 수는 없을까?(개정판)』 서울: 부흥과개혁사, 2003.

부이치치, 닉, 카나에 부이치치. 『닉 부이치치 부부의 한계를 껴안는 결혼』 정성묵 옮김. 서울: 두란노, 2017.

사이먼 후미. 『연애론』 이소영 옮김. 고양: 봄고양이, 2016.

송웅달. 『900일간의 폭풍 사랑』 서울: 김영사, 2007.

웨스트민스터 총회. 『원문을 그대로 번역한 웨스트민스터 소교리문답(영한대조)』 권율 옮김. 서울: 세움북스, 2018.

유해무. 『개혁교의학』 고양: 크리스챤다이제스트, 1997.

이애경. 『기다리다 죽겠어요』 서울: 터치북스, 2012.

이재욱. 『나의 선택과 하나님의 뜻』 서울: 좋은씨앗, 2019.

최유수. 『사랑의 목격』 서울: 허밍버드, 2020.

▒ WEBSITES

Merriam-Wester. "vision," https://www.merriam-webster.com/dictionary/vision (accessed January 8, 2022).

Miller, Korin. "What Is Sexual Grooming? Here's What Experts Say About This Manipulative Behavior." https://www.health.com/relationships/what-is-grooming-sexual (accessed January 8, 2022).

Sternberg, Robert J. "Triangular Theory of Love." http://www.robertjsternberg.com/love (accessed January 8, 2022).

Texas For Marriage. "6 Best Traditional Protestant Wedding Vows, Example #1." https://texasformarriage.org/6-best-traditional-protestant-wedding-vows (accessed January 8, 2022).

Westminster Assembly. *The Westminster Confession of Faith & Larger and Shorter Catechisms In Modern English Including the Creeds* on this site: http://sheffieldpres.org.uk/Westminster_Standards.pdf

네이버 바이브. "남자의 첫사랑은 무덤까지 간다." https://vibe.naver.com/track/800442 (2022년 1월 8일 검색).

선교한국. "선교한국의 사명." http://missionkorea.org/선교한국운동 (2022년 1월 8일 검색).

신상목. "[역경의 열매] 김영길 〈5〉: 사진으로만 본 신붓감과 1년 편지교제 끝 결혼." 《국민일보 미션라이프》 2016년 6월 16일. http://news.kmib.co.kr/article/view.asp?arcid=0923566809&code=23111513&cp=nv.

유원정. "'힐링캠프' 닉 부이치치, 아내와 러브 스토리도 '뭉클'." 《CBS노컷뉴스》 2013년 6월 18일. https://www.nocutnews.co.kr/news/1052676.